# The Faith Of A Skeptic...

## Seeking Truth and Balance In Religion and Politics

## Thomas W. Lentz

### Foreword by Joseph M. Bearson

THE FAITH OF A SKEPTIC

FIRST EDITION
Copyright © 2018
by CSS Publishing Co., Inc.
Published by CSS Publishing Company, Inc., Lima, Ohio 45807. All rights
reserved. No part of this publication may be reproduced in any manner
whatsoever without the prior permission of the publisher, except in the
case of brief quotations embodied in critical articles and reviews. Inqui-
ries should be addressed to: CSS Publishing Company, Inc., Permissions
Department, 5450 N. Dixie Highway, Lima, Ohio 45807.

**Library of Congress Cataloging-in-Publication Data**

2018054566

For more information about CSS Publishing Company resources, visit our website at www.csspub.com, email us at csr@csspub.com, or call
(800) 241-4056.

e-book:
ISBN-13: 978-0-7880-4084-9
ISBN-10: 0-7880-4084-7

ISBN-13: 978-0-7880-4083-2
ISBN-10: 0-7880-4083-9                    PRINTED IN USA

# Contents

Preface ............................................................. 5

Foreword ........................................................... 8

Introduction ......................................................11

1. Don't Be Too Sure… .......................................17

2. Chase Life............................................................29

3. The Sacred And The Sensual ......................43

4. Cry At The Birth Rejoice At The Death ........................49

5. Seeking Truth… ............................................59

6. What The World Needs Now… ...............................67

7. Faith And Doubt ..........................................77

8. You Are Dying, But Not Right Now… ..........................99

9. Audacious............................................................ 111

10. A Discovery That Changed History ....................... 129

11. Ecclesiastical Humor – Censored........................... 137

12. Doing The Right Thing, When The Right Thing Is Hard To Do ...... 149

13. Restoring Intellectual Challenge.......................... 155

14. Dangerous Convictions… ................................ 177

15. How Normal Are You? ...................................... 187

16. Duel To The Death ........................................ 197

17. Rules For Survival ........................................ 217

18. What Is Piety?........................................... 223

19. Generations ................................................ 231

20. Varieties Of Worship: From Snakes To Strychnine .................. 239

21. The Final Breath… ........................................ 247

22. Last Page ................................................. 251

# Preface

When I drove down the long lane to the country farm where I had been buying eggs, I had another mission in mind. As I approached the farm house I noticed a girl of ten or twelve, barefoot and wearing a long dress, struggling to push a hand-powered lawn mower through tall grass. I got out of the car and greeted the nine-year-old boy who had walked over to look at my van. He noticed the Florida license plate and asked, "Do you have a lot of alligators down there?" Although he was short for his age, I had learned from previous visits that in addition to a bright intellect and unrelenting curiosity, he was already a seasoned farmer. I had seen him driving a team of large draft horses out of a barn, pulling a disc to work the soil in a nearby field.

I asked for his mother who soon appeared in a long gray dress and bonnet. She was slender and attractive and did not look old enough to be the mother of twelve children. She carried my two dozen brown eggs — $1.25 a dozen — in her hands. After completing the transaction, I asked her if it would be possible to speak to her husband. She disappeared and her tall, gaunt Amish husband came to the door with a friendly smile. I briefly described my interest in philosophy and religion. I told him that for many years I had admired the Amish way of life and had helped an Amish farmer in Holmes Country, Ohio, find a repair for his manual typewriter. Eventually, I got around to my intended purpose for speaking to him.

"Would it be possible for me to come and live with your family for a month, in order to experience the way you approach life and faith, 'to be in the world, but not of the world?' I would, of course, pay rent and work and worship along with you and your family."

I have since learned that this request is not all that uncommon. We are called seekers, who have developed a profound interest in a culture which has discovered how not only to survive, but to thrive without the modern conveniences of electricity, indoor plumbing, internet, and transportation that we have become so dependent upon.

One of the characteristics I admire is the Amish emphasis upon family and community. Many Amish communities, which approve of propane gas for interior lights, restrict it to family areas — the kitchen, living room, or dining area. This encourages families to gather in the same area in the evening for reading and conversation, rather than retreating to separate rooms in the house. Evidence of this community spirit is shown in the neighborhood barn raisings, and the outpouring of food, money, and labor that is provided when a family loses an adult or child.

Living simply is not exclusive to the Amish or any particular religious orientation. For many years our family has drawn inspiration from a couple who retreated from their jobs in society, bought a ten acre farm, and made the conscious decision to live frugally, even below the so-called "poverty line." This had nothing to do with religious conviction; in fact they turned from organized religion in favor of agnosticism. They have a deep-seated desire to adopt an agrarian life, to respect the land and to take pleasure in the work of their hands. Renouncing wealth, they read voraciously and, unlike the Amish, most of whom don't vote in public elections, they have strong political convictions.

Whenever my wife and I begin to feel that we are becoming too materialistic, too attached to our possessions, or too eager to seek entertainment by 'pleasure shopping,' we say to each other, "It's time to get our Jan and Andy fix."

✠ ✠ ✠

*The Faith of a Skeptic* reflects the influence that associations such as these have impressed on me through the years. They have taught me to be less judgmental, to ask more questions, and to seek truth rather than certainty. But I confess, that 'being less judgmental' is a daily battle, a discipline that I have not mastered. Yet those who *have* developed the capacity to overcome the natural human instinct to become self-righteously judgmental are the models whom I most admire.

Throughout these chapters I have promoted the wisdom of searching for common ground, which includes listening to those with whom we disagree. In our multi-cultural society we work beside those whose religious views are different from our own. We live next door to folks who voted for a different president or follow a different kind of faith. These differences can be irritating; but they can also lead to opportunity. They can provide an exciting challenge to find out why he is a Baptist or a Buddhist, why she voted for Hillary or Donald — to engage in the stimulating exploration of human diversity.

Observance of human behavior soon reveals that there is no direct connection between morality and religious affiliation. People who worship God do not have a monopoly on ethical instruction or behavior. All we have to do is look inward to realize how far short we fall from the tenets of our faith. And when we analyze the community of faith we find frequent disconnection between faithful worship and compassionate concern for others. Bigotry exists in some churches. Immoral acts are sometimes committed by ecclesiastical leaders. Unlike the Good Samaritan, our compassion often extends only to those who look like us, think like us, vote like us, or worship as we do. On the other hand, we often find examples of compassion, forgiveness, and tolerance among those who have no apparent religious affiliation.

Skepticism keeps us humble. It encourages us to search for common values, and in the end to realize that we can achieve greater happiness when we discover in our unexalted humanity that none of us is any better than the other. As the Italian proverb says, "At the end of the game the king and the pawn go into the same box."

Tom Lentz

# Foreword

Endeavoring to find truth is a tricky bit of business even in the most simplistic of situations, but when engaging in religious thought, it can be an absolutely disturbing struggle. The entire process begins with the inevitable doubt that stems from critical thinking about the meaning of existence, often ending with frustration and cynicism, the curse of the defrocked idealist.

The position of the skeptic incorporates the by-product of our doubts. Some people, perhaps wisely but perhaps not, choose to beg the issue of faith and safely retire into the waiting arms of informal agnosticism. Woody Allen's discomfort with his related struggles is reflected in one of his film character's descriptive reference to his own relationship to God as a "member of the loyal opposition." Others accept the teachings of a particular religion and commit their faith without question. Interestingly, the self-avowed atheist most often must apply skepticism to his own conclusion, if nothing else than on a purely existential basis.

Dealing with the perplexing problem of absolute truth has been found at the heart of commentary by thinkers throughout time. Some operate with great resolve and assurance by employing their own firmly established concept of verity. But, is absolute truth akin to an ambiguous Rorschach blot and, as such, subject to human interpretation? Interestingly, the author's divinity studies were made at Yale University where one finds the prominent motto *Lux et Veritas* (Truth and Light).

To a starving person mere nutrition is happiness. To a sick one, a day of feeling well is happiness. A strong dose of mind-altering drugs might be happiness to a spoiled rock star seeking kicks beyond the largess of money, fame and doting followers. Isn't that all about need fulfillment and, is that what one really means by being happy? This is a subject deserving ample time under the author's microscope.

One is invited to open the floodgates in an investigation of the confines of "normal" behavior. Questions arise about just how arbitrarily 'normal" is defined in our society and the subject becomes strongly relevant by contrasting the various overviews posed by religion, psychology, cultural imperatives, et al. The author holds the readers' hands and invites open-mindedness in marching through various prevailing perspectives.

The ponderous elephant called politics prominently stands in the center of the skeptic's chamber. Contemporary issues resonate deafeningly and dominate the headlines of current news stories, editorials, and feature material through the media. Quite naturally, this area does not escape the sharp focus of the author.

Caveats concerning dangerous convictions and their implications beg to be developed and exposed by the clear-eyed skeptic. Moving from historical events to a relevant overview of presently vital concerns, an insightful analysis serves as a key component in the author's bottomless tool kit.

Piety had been traditionally defined in terms of duty, reverence, and virtuous devotion. Oddly, over time the word has often been associated with the description of elements of sham and hypocrisy. Understandably, these contrary perceptions and the reasons for them cannot escape the watchful skeptical eye.

Tom Lentz, the author of *The Faith of a Skeptic*, approaches his intellectual struggles with a supple mind, a researcher's zeal, cogent observational skills, a keen intuition based upon the enlightenment of age and experience, and a charming sense of humor. His willingness to parse the implications and variations of faith provides him with a rare facility to examine the subject using both ends of the telescope, peering at macro and micro issues. The result is a provocative and highly instructive treatment of a universal and eternal subject rife with mysteries that have eluded the mind-tumbling of many serious scholars. Here we find a virtual handbook for an intellectual journeyman, of any age, in search of ever evasive truth.

Alternately, Lentz employs both fine point and broad brushes where appropriate to create an artistic landscape of contemporary issues. Problems and paradoxes pertaining to cultural imperatives are handled deftly with keen investigations, genuine sincerity, and, most often, intriguing wit. The result is a feast of delicacies for the palates of those who have struggled with ironies encountered by searching for endorsements of basic faith. One finds here a plethora of "aha moments" along with the dissection of as many intriguingly timeless questions.

Finally, if an alien, without a clue about religious thought, lands on earth from Mars, burdensome levels of information about hundreds of this planet's institutionalized religions and the branches of each could be presented for educational consumption. It would be most disappointing and unfortunate if *The Faith of a Skeptic* was not offered for significant consideration. Even, non-Martians will find that Thomas Lentz offers brain candy to ingest while wandering through the inquisitive minefield of critical thinking.

Joseph M. Bearson, Professor Emeritus,
Eckerd College

# Introduction

My awareness of human interaction began to take shape the moment I released my first infant cry. It drew a response that delivered nourishment. I was held. I was fed. After a few years I was given instructions: told when I had to go to bed or take a nap. Demands were made: what I could or could not do. I learned that defying those instructions would result in angry words and sometimes painful punishment.

Along the way I began to take notice of behavior in our family that pointed to something ethereal, at first incomprehensible: we bowed our heads and talked, but not to each other. The words were directed to something, or someone, who was not visibly present. This occurred when we sat down to eat a meal. At night before I fell asleep my father would come into my bedroom and say those words, while we both closed our eyes and folded our hands. It planted a seed: the idea, the belief, that the things asked for in those moments — sleeping through the night, staying healthy, or being loved even when I had been bad — might be granted by someone, some unseen power that was important to observe; of such significance that even my protective earthly father bowed in obeisance to that power. As I grew older I was taught that if I did not pay heed to that power, there could be pernicious consequences. I learned about hell.

The idea was that this power, this unseen deity, could make my life better; but it was conditional: I had to pay attention to it, "pray" to it, and carry out certain expectations in order to receive the benefits that this deity could confer. Stories were read and told to me that conveyed a new vocabulary: God, salvation, Jesus, heaven, sin, worship. It was impressed upon me that the importance of these could not be overstated. Awareness and observation of them was associated with the degree to which life was valued. "For the wages of sin is death, but the gift of God is eternal life in Christ Jesus our Lord" (Romans 6:23).

In second grade I met a girl. I had a schoolboy crush on her. She was associated with a place where they had a different approach to the deity. She was called a Catholic, and I learned that there was something different about that association. Something of which to be wary. Her deity was described in a different way from ours — maybe not as effective. Something about this did not seem right.

In fifth grade I had a classmate whose parents denied — gasp — that this deity even existed. I was warned about him. It was something to be a little frightened about.

In another part of the world a child was learning that there is one true deity; and it was different from ours. It was named the Supreme Spirit, or Brahman. And still elsewhere children were discovering multiple deities, Shinto gods, called *kami*. Were these children bad? Could they be condemned for living and dying without ever becoming aware of my deity — Creator God…and his son? The first seeds of skepticism were sewn.

Would my deity tolerate these other spirits? The Bible says that *he* is jealous and will permit no other gods to be acknowledged. In fact *he* advocates the violent suppression of any competitive spiritual representations. The second half of the Book was more tolerant and less violent. "Do not judge, or you too will be judged."

As my awareness of the world expanded, I began hearing about beliefs that were completely alien to my understanding of our deity, God. There was Buddhism; and Jainism, known as Jain Dharma — a religion that existed hundreds of years before the birth of Jesus. Jainism taught that the universe was eternal and had no need of a creator; salvation is achieved by perfection through successive lives — rebirths. What, I had to ask, would my God think of that?

Skepticism deepened and deflated my comfortable certitude. I began to leave room for other faiths, other perceptions of how the deity is described. My skepticism implied a more humble posture: maybe I don't know as much as I thought I did; maybe there is a bigger picture; maybe there is much more than what I have been taught. I started to climb down from the plateau of certainty and look into the face of a Catholic, a Buddhist, an atheist, a Muslim.

I had a flash of insight: I had fallen into a trap that my deity had warned against: the conviction that my beliefs were superior to others; my picture of how the world operates more accurate. How could I have skipped so lightly over one of the most warned about human errors: hubris — exaggerated pride and over-inflated confidence? I had to admit that I did not have an unobstructed view of truth, and perhaps never would.

✛ ✛ ✛

Skepticism helps me become more tolerant of others: less vehement and impassioned when I encounter opposition. Religion. Politics. We form alliances based upon the degree of commonality we share in these two areas. Churches invite those who will confess a common creed. Fellowship is granted among those who support the same political platform.

We identify as "believer" or "non-believer"; as Democrat or Republican. These identities are capable of determining our closest friendships.

I checked into my hotel room in Chicago just as the cleaning lady was finishing. The television was tuned to Fox News and Sean Hannity. I asked her if she watched any other news channels. No, she said she only watched Fox News. I asked, don't you wonder what the other people are thinking? I don't care what anyone else thinks, she said as she pushed the cleaning cart of the room. Apparently many watch the news for confirmation, not information.

This observation encourages me to be a skeptic. Skepticism breaks down stubborn intransigence. Skepticism builds bridges. It crosses over the divide. When I become convinced that I am right, it warns, don't be too sure. It encourages me to listen before I condemn.

Political division has destroyed friendships, distanced family members, and driven some to violent acts. Skepticism whispers 'stop and listen; you might be just a little bit wrong.'

"We must try to find a way to see citizens on the other side as cousins who are...never our mortal enemies" (John Adams). My creed is the renunciation of certitude, which is the cause of most human conflict.

Our founding fathers struggled for many days and long hours to create a system of government that would be tolerant of opposing ideas. In the end Thomas Jefferson wrote to John Adams, "That you and I differ in our idea of the best form of government is well known to us both; but we have differed as friends should do, respecting the purity of each other's motives."

This is the spirit that brought decency and honor to the democracy with which we have been endowed. I hope that what I have written will serve this spirit of democracy.

I started investing in the stock market during my senior year in high school. I used money from my paper route and numerous small jobs. I skimmed the newspapers, and I listened for hot tips. I bought Standard Oil of Indiana, United States Steel, Monsanto Chemical, and Kodak. Like many novice investors I bought the stock when everyone else had bought it, and sold it when the news of negative earnings quarter dropped the stock to below where I had bought it.

So I started looking for characteristics that would improve my timing: cheap stocks with low price/earnings multiples. That's how I learned that some stocks are cheap for a reason. They have no future. They won't grow in price.

Within a few years I was analyzing several other factors: size, value, profitability, quality, momentum. Whereas investing based on one factor alone had led to mixed results, my small portfolio performed better when I chose stocks that qualified according to several of these factors. I made better judgments when I no longer chose a stock based on only one or two factors.

In similar fashion the judgments I made about people changed with experience. I found that it took more than a pretty face to enjoy a girl on a date. It helped if she had a sense of humor and a positive spirit.

When I set out to write about our religious and political affiliations I began to realize how dominant these two factors have become in determining whom we choose as friends and whom we eliminate. A fellow may have served the country as a war hero, but if he says he doesn't like Donald Trump, that may be enough to disqualify his value to a serious Trump supporter.

A woman who is kind and loving, who gives to many charitable causes and devotes her life to her children may be rejected by her "Christian" neighbor, because the woman is a Muslim.

These two factors — religion and politics — weigh heavily in our judgments. My objective in advocating skepticism is to enlarge our perspective of each person's value: render judgment according to more than one or two factors. Seek the flesh and blood human being behind the façade of religious (or non-religious) and political affiliation.

Some factors are strong disqualifiers for a stock, like bankruptcy. So too, there are certain human disqualifiers: bigotry and narcissism are almost certain to preclude the capacity for friendship, because those who fit these descriptions seem incapable of considering any but their own suppositions. They seem incapable of self-analysis or skepticism.

✠ ✠ ✠

I am grateful to readers who receive this in the way that is intended: as an invitation to consider a point of view that is alien and in some cases even distasteful to your own; to question your resistance and ponder whether any truth might possibly exist beyond the borders of your own beliefs. I don't expect too many to embrace the challenge. But then, I am a skeptic.

# Chapter 1

# Don't Be Too Sure...

Bumper sticker: *Intelligent people are curious.*
*Idiots are sure.*
Skeptic: a person inclined to question or doubt
all accepted opinions.

At a time when basic facts are disputed, truth becomes obliterated by ridicule and empty rhetoric. Reason and rationalization are scrambled. The intention of faith is disputed; expounded with self-serving definitions by sanctimonious Pharisees. The content of scripture is interpreted literally by some, metaphorically by others. And both sides declare their beliefs with complete certainty...without a shred of skepticism. How do you know who has a better handle on truth?

Religious conviction can be the cause of more conflict than compromise. Historically it has been the impetus for war as well as the inspiration for peacemaking.

Questions separate the undoubting from the skeptic.

When did God first exist?

How do you know there is only one God?

Did all human life descend from Adam and Eve?

Is abortion murder?

Is suicide breaking a commandment?

Is one church denomination more biblically faithful than another?

Will non-believers go to hell? How about Muslims or those who have never heard of Jesus?

Are the body and blood of Jesus present in the sacrament of communion?

Can prayer prevent accidents or heal a sick person?

Should deviled eggs be served at church potlucks?

Okay, I'm kidding about that last one, but it's comparable to the *reductio ad absurdum* of medieval scholasticism, which debated the number of angels who can dance on the head of a pin.

The question of how many angels can stand on the head of a pin referred to the imagery of ecclesiastical clerics wasting time on topics that are of no practical value. The absurdity of certain current day minutiae is illustrated by the imaginary debate over whether deviled eggs should be allowed at church potlucks. The answer: only if they are balanced with angel food cake. (Don't take that too seriously.)

Religion has sometimes been the source of more censure than charity. Evangelical Christians question whether atheists and Muslims are beyond redemption. Biblical literalists claim that all human life descended from Adam and Eve. Emotion overpowers reason: like the abortion critic who bombs abortion clinics and murders doctors for performing abortions. Logic be damned.

Religion has been the impetus for as much conflict as it has compassion. The early centuries of Christianity were often marked with irrational zeal and cruel treatment. By the fifth century monks were subjected to hundreds of rules as simple as eating a cucumber at the right time. Punishments ranged from brutal flogging to pouring molten lead down the throat.

Vicious attacks could be perpetrated on anyone who did not share a particular Christian belief. Those who were "blind" to true religion might have their eyes gouged out. One bishop had his tongue cut out for preaching supposed falsehoods.

In the fifth century Christian zealots took pious pride in tearing down the statues of pagan gods. The naked Aphrodite statue with her fullsome bottom and naked breasts was considered a work of evil; after all, the statue might incite lustful thoughts in one who cast eyes on her. Bands of Christians destroyed temples and bathhouses where the devil might be lurking.[1]

Old Testament precepts applied to every phase of living from the moment one arose in the morning until retiring for the night. Like a badgering overseer, clerics kept their subjects under the constant threat of criticism, punishment or death. The Old Testament holds nothing in reserve when speaking of the wrath of God, his threats, his punishments, the fire and brimstone he rains down, the illnesses he is capable of sending, and the eternal punishment he brings to the unrepentant.

No other religious debate is more incongruous than that which attempts to describe the nature a supreme being. The God who is portrayed by Mosaic Law in the Old Testament is decisive and vindictive. His temper is vicious and unrelenting. Examples emerge in the opening chapters of the Bible where it is recorded that God killed Judah's firstborn son, "because he was wicked." No other explanation is given (Genesis 38:7). But father Judah wanted his blood line to continue, so he commanded his other son, Onan, to "sleep with your brother's wife and fulfill your duty to her as a brother-in-law..." (Genesis 38:8). Onan, obedient young man that he was, went ahead and slept with his brother's wife. But he was not keen on getting her pregnant, so he "spilled his semen on the ground" to prevent the dead brother from having offspring, which would diminish his inheritance. The Almighty was not happy about this sly deception, so "the Lord put him to death also."

From that story the word *onanism* entered our English dictionary, defined as "coitus interruptus, improper emission of seed," hereafter also included among the multitude of sins catalogued in Hebrew Law. And from these stories we are led to assume that one would be ill-advised to provoke this vicious Hebrew God.

If a convert were introduced to Christianity through the reading of Leviticus, the third book of the Bible, he might turn and flee in dismay. This third book of Moses spells out detailed lists of regulations concerning diet, laws about ritual sacrifice, laws of purity, and laws of motherhood, immorality, and religious festivals. Examples: an animal brought for a burnt offering must be a male without defect; a grain offering must be of fine flour. All flying insects must be avoided except those that have jointed legs for hopping on the ground, for example, a locust or grasshopper. A woman who gives birth to a son remains ceremoniously unclean for seven days, and for fourteen days after the birth of a daughter. At the end of that time, she must bring a one-year-old lamb to the priest for a burnt offering, as well as a young pigeon for a sin offering.

A detailed list spelled out those with whom sexual intercourse was prohibited and provides a vivid indication of the primitive nature of this ancient society. It included any family member or blood relative: your mother, your sister, your father's wife or sister, your brother's wife, any woman during her menstrual period, or any animal.

The brutality of the Israelite culture becomes evident when one reads that there had to be a prohibition against sacrificing children to Molek (an Israelite god). Numerous transgressions required the death penalty. Anyone who cursed his father or his mother must be put to death, as well as anyone who committed adultery. If a man or woman had sex with an animal he or she must be put to death, as well as the animal. These and dozens more highly detailed proscriptions fill the pages of Leviticus. (Assuredly, they had nothing on our busy legislators: there are 20,000 laws on our books today just to regulate the use of guns.)

Woe to God's chosen people who disobeyed his laws: if you will not listen to me…then I will bring on you sudden terror and diseases; fever will destroy your sight. I will punish you seven times over. I will break down your stubborn pride. If you remain hostile and refuse to listen to me, I will send wild animals against you, and they will rob you of your children (Leviticus 26:14 — 25). These harsh punishments were apparently necessary to elevate the culture of tribal bands from barbarism.

The New Testament introduces a more kindhearted God; but still a God who "opposes the proud, and shows favor to the humble" (James 4:6). More compassionate maybe, but also a God who will not let us forget that we are far from perfect.

The New Testament Christian is never allowed to feel free of guilt. It is inescapable. The imposition of guilt is a critical control mechanism of religious doctrine. Those who think that conversion shelters them from guilt fool themselves. They become the self-righteous critics; the cranky gossips who delight in tattling about the vices of their neighbors. They see the speck in their neighbor's eye and ignore the 2x4 in their own eye.

True conversion sharpens this consciousness of guilt. "For I do not do the good I want to do, but the evil I do not want to do — this I keep on doing...Although I want to do good, evil is right there with me...What a wretched man I am! Who will rescue me from this body that is subject to death?" (Romans 7:24).

Zealots find ways to complicate the simplest commandments; to observe a certain ritual which might ameliorate the remorse of guilt. Theologians deliberate the nature of God's presence in the sacrament of Holy Communion. There's not much help for them on that subject in the Bible. Traditional Roman Catholicism taught that the bread and wine of communion become, in actuality, the body and blood of Jesus Christ, a metamorphosis called transubstantiation. Protestant theology modified that belief: the body and blood of Jesus Christ are present in the sacrament, although the substance of the elements themselves does not change. While scholars debated these arcane doctrines, their followers lost very little sleep over them. A curse of the human condition is to search for ways to complicate the simple.

French author and Nobel Prize winner, Andre Paul Gide wrote "Believe those who are seeking the truth; run from the one who has found it." That's another way of admonishing skepticism. Truth can be elusive.

When brought before Pontius Pilate, Jesus claimed "Everyone on the side of truth listens to me." To which Pilate responded, "What is truth?" Strangely, the Bible doesn't say that Jesus gave any answer to this question. A footnote in the NIV Bible attempts to explain it as either joking (as in 'what does it matter?') or, that if Pilate was serious he may have meant 'it's not easy to find truth.' But maybe Jesus was exemplifying greater wisdom by ignoring the question.

"Knowledge consists in the search for truth. It is not the search for certainty." (Australian-British philosopher Karl Popper)

When faith becomes bound by iron clad conviction, it shuns skepticism and is suspicious of questions. A skeptic listens to disagreement and sees it as an opportunity to gain insight into the diversity of human reasoning; an occasion to see inside the mind of someone different. Skepticism requires courage. It is a warning against false security. Doctrinal piety can lead to vindictive self-righteousness.

Theologian Paul Tillich wrote, 'Sometimes I think it is my mission to bring faith to the faithless, and doubt to the faithful." We must not be so adamant about our religious suppositions that we become judgmental and incapable of listening to someone who follows a different creed. Skepticism welcomes cognitive challenge, possibly even a corrective insight.

"Surely…we cannot imagine any certainty that is not tinged with doubt, or any assurance that is not assailed by some anxiety" wrote John Calvin, theologian and reformer during the Protestant Reformation.

Nothing invites an argument like a discussion about politics or religion. We entertain a fierce certitude about our beliefs in these two areas. We feel instantly alienated from those who criticize our propositions. We develop bonds of friendship with those who support our religious and political ideas.

The avowed atheist is unlikely to claim a Baptist as his best friend. The lady who campaigned door-to-door for

Hillary Clinton isn't about to schedule a weekly lunch date with her neighbor who chaired the local Women for Trump campaign. We are likely to talk only with like-minded individuals, so we can avoid listening to the other side. Our animal instinct drives us to run with our own pack — with those who think and believe as we do.

My dental hygienist, Debra, poured out her lament as I sat in the chair with my mouth open, unable to respond — the ideal captive audience. She told me that she is no longer able to have a peaceful phone conversation with her mother. It breaks her heart, but each time she calls her mother — four states away from Florida to West Virginia coal mining country– the subject of the president comes up. Her mother asserts that God appointed Donald Trump to be the president of the United States.

"How do you know that," Debra asked her mother?

"You really should read *The Trump Prophecies*," her mother told her. "It proves that God has chosen Donald Trump to be our president."

I searched for the book and found it prominently displayed in a small Ohio village library. *The Trump Prophecies* is a passionately written book by Mark Taylor and Mary Colbert. Mark Taylor began having visions in which God appeared to him. "I instantly knew it was God," he said. Taylor took the message of the vision to a "certified dream interpreter associated with John Paul Jackson's Streams Ministries International." The interpreter told Mark that the vision he had experienced was a "visitation from the Lord." Taylor later declared that it was the same kind of vision that occurred to Moses.

A few years ago as Taylor was watching Fox News, he saw an interview with Donald Trump and suddenly was struck "by the inspiration of God (so) that my spirit tingled with anticipation. From out of the blue, I started to discern an odd sensation of certainty, as if I were about to be told something that had already been solidly ordained in the spiritual realm....And then, like a ringing in my spiritual ears, came the Lord's disclosure. *You are hearing the voice of a president.*"

At that moment he knew it was time to "pick up my pen and obey the directive the Lord had given me…as I kept my pen moving, more words were forming into complete sentences, and I wrote with confidence as the Lord led.

*The Spirit of God says, I have chosen this man, Donald Trump, for such a time as this. For as Benjamin Netanyahu is to Israel, so shall this man be to the United States of America!*[2]

"How," Debra asked me as she picked away at my teeth," can I have a reasonable conversation when my mother believes that Donald Trump was sent by God to be our president?" I couldn't answer with my mouth still wide open, so she went on: "I asked my mother if she ever heard President Trump say that he would build a wall and that Mexico would pay for it. "He didn't say Mexico would pay for it," she told me. "That's fake news. I heard Tucker Carlson say so."[3]

When she was done and I could use my mouth to speak, I said to her, "Are you aware of what President Trump calls 'fake news?' In an interview with Lesley Stahl he asked her, 'do you know why I call it fake news? I do it so that when you write negative stories about me no one will believe you."

Beliefs (opinions) become fossilized into convictions. Opposing beliefs become a threat. Samuel Johnson said, "Every man who attacks my belief…makes me uneasy; and I am angry with him who makes me uneasy."

I am thankful for those friends and associates with whom I can discuss the policies and politics of President Trump without descending into angry rhetoric and bitterness. There are traits about the president that make him an easy target. But I have friends who are Trump supporters. They have calmly listened to my opposition and then explained their own reasoning. I extend the olive branch to anyone who is capable of discussing differences in a civil manner. When a Facebook message simple-mindedly claims "if you don't like the president of our country, choose a different country," it does not lead to meaningful dialogue. It is simply taunting and divisive.

A doctor confessed to me in 2016 that he would vote for Trump; he has since become more evasive. A friend and neighbor told me that he would hold his nose and vote for Trump. Two fellow business executives maintain their support for the Trump administration. These are individuals whom I respect. I consider their views. They listen to my concerns. This is how American democracy should work. In later chapters of this book I share space for their views. There is hope for democracy when two opposing sides continue to talk to each other. Faith involves the willingness to be a skeptic even about one's own beliefs.

"He who knows only his own side of the case knows little of that. His reasons may be good, and no one may have been able to refute them. But if he is equally unable to refute the reasons on the opposite side, if he does not so much as know what they are, he has no ground for preferring either opinion." (John Stuart Mill)

Throughout the course of my student years at Wittenberg University I worked the night shift at International Harvester Company. During our coffee breaks I started discussing politics with a co-worker. He and his wife were a childless couple in their forties who owned a small farm a few miles from the factory. He was a Kennedy Democrat. I was a swaggering Republican college student. After our heated debates, Clarence would break the tension by saying, "Come on, Tommy my boy; let's come out of our corners and see if we can meet somewhere in the middle here." He was a master arbitrator. After a few more coffee break exchanges he must have seen some hope for me. He invited me to live and work on his farm for free room and board. "Let's see who can plant the straightest row," he said. "If you can beat me, I'll become a Republican." It was a grueling routine: night shift, followed by his wife's breakfast of pancakes and eggs, three hours sleep, and then classes at Wittenberg. On weekends and days that I had no scheduled classes, we worked together on farm chores. He never did have to keep his vow to become a Republican.

After living with this couple for several months, I started paying more attention to the Kennedy administration. Although JFK, a Boston-bred urbanite, probably knew less about farming than any other political candidate, he relied heavily on his advisors, especially Ted Sorensen, whose father had been born in a Nebraska sod house. It may have been Sorensen who influenced Kennedy to declare that "The family farm should remain the backbone of American agriculture...the decline in agricultural income is the number one domestic problem in the United States."

Although I was the beneficiary of a formal education, I sometimes consider that I may have been learning equally important lessons about life and human nature from Clarence and his wife. The Dalai Lama taught that when you cultivate the right attitude, your political adversaries are your best spiritual teachers, because they provide you with the opportunity to develop tolerance, patience and understanding.

## Notes

1 — Nixey, Catherine, *The Darkening Ave: The Christian Destruction of the Classical World*, (2017, Pan Macmillan, London), p. 223.

2 — Taylor, Mark and Mary Colbert, *The Trump Prophecies: The Astonishing True Story of the Man Who Saw Tomorrow...and What He says Is Coming Next,* (2017, B&N Dayton, Beavercreek).

3 — During the presidential campaign in 2016, Donald Trump repeatedly claimed that the border wall would be paid for by Mexico, not by American taxpayers. Fake News, however, is a new reality we live with. In mid-2016 Craig Silverman was investigating news sources and noticed a steady stream of made-up stories that were coming out of the small town of Veles in the Eastern European Republic of Macedonia. Silverman investigated and discovered over 140 fake news websites which

were attracting millions of hits on Facebook. The US presidential election, and especially Donald Trump, was the hot topic. This turned out to be the source of such made-up headlines as "FBI Agent Suspected in Hillary Email Leaks Found Dead in Apparent Suicide," and "Pope Francis Endorses Donald Trump for President." BBC News reported that Hillary Clinton used the term "fake news" in a speech, when she referred to "the epidemic of malicious fake news and false propaganda that has flooded social media over the past year." She was undoubtedly referring to the concocted report that the Clintons were operating a sex ring out of a pizza parlor. It became known as "pizzagate."

# Chapter 2

# Chase Life......

*The world breaks everyone and afterward many are strong in the broken places. But those that will not break it kills. It kills the very good and the very gentle and the very brave impartially.*
Ernest Hemingway, *A Farewell to Arms,* 1929

It is human nature to challenge authority, including the authority of the Bible and religious doctrine. But when death dropped in with its hard, cold reality, it forced me to ask deeper questions about the meaning of existence. It jolted me from the mundane tasks of grocery shopping, doctor's appointments, or stock market research. Preoccupation with daily living precludes thoughtful reflection on the significance of ethnic diversity, cyber warfare, global justice, death...God. Life is already too complicated to have time for facing east in a lotus position and contemplating why I am here. But death and the stark realization of impermanence become unavoidable: the diagnosis of incurable cancer, the death of a child, the abandonment of a husband or wife. These events sink us first into hopeless despair...and then deep reflection. What brings life its meaning?

My daily routine involves faith in myself, not in an external, unseen deity. But death or emotional pain cause me to retreat to the same reflection as the young Harvard student who wrote in his diary, "Oh that the Lord would teach me how to think and how to choose." (This quote was used in the book *College: What It Was, Is and Should Be* by Andrew Delbanco.) This search for meaning is not mine alone. It places me in fellowship with centuries of skeptics who have searched for something more than a material world. Death shocks us out of our complacency, and arouses a longing to explore the mystery of life. Failure or rejection humble us and guide us to probe the enigma of spiritual reality.

Because Christianity has held up the value of self-sacrifice as the highest good, it has been tolerant of death. According to Christian doctrine, death, rather than being a metaphysical mystery, is what gives life its meaning. In previous generations, it was not the doctor who was called when death was imminent, but the priest who came to prepare the dying person for the afterlife. Medical science, on the other hand, pictures death as a challenge, a technical glitch that has to be solved by an antibiotic or a kidney transplant. The aim of medical science is the extension of life, not a concession to death.

"What is the Christian view of death and the afterlife?" This was the theme of an essay I was instructed to write for the professor in a graduate school theology seminar. My sanguine conclusion may have sounded like the Christian counterpart of Islamic *Shahada*. I suggested that death can be witnessed as a reprieve from the perplexing froth and frustration of earthly existence. It is nothing to fear for the Christian, I surmised. "Jesus said, 'I am the resurrection and the life. He who believes in me will live, even though he dies; and whoever lives and believes in me will never die'" (John 11:25-26).

I concluded the essay with the bold assertion that death is a glorious beginning for a believer. "For me to live is Christ, and to die is gain," Saint Paul wrote in his letter to the church in Philippi (Philippians 1:21). From this perspective death is translated as either "the great adventure," or "eternal rest."

Well, maybe...if you're looking at the question from an arms-length view of theology. But only a few of us are so analytical as to accept it without some degree of sorrow or fear, some dread, some apprehension of doubt when it strikes close to home.

Biblical literature teaches that earthly life is an inferior fragment of our ultimate purpose. Rather than to be feared, dying is said to diminish the illusion of our self-importance.

It reveals that we are misguided when we put too much importance on our earthly survival and accomplishments. It teaches that we must let go of the security we get from accumulation of wealth and possessions: "Do not store up for yourselves treasures on earth...." But regardless of these teachings we often find it difficult to get rid of our "things" as we get older. They provide a sense of security. They represent memories that we don't want to lose. We fill our closets with mementos of these times past.

## Death, Rejection, Abandonment

We are able to accept more easily the death of a person who has dwelt on this earth at least seventy years, which is a normal life span in biblical terms. "The years of our life are threescore and ten" (Psalm 90:10).

At the funeral service of my 99-year-old grandmother, the preacher bellowed from the pulpit, "Today is a day of victory for Ida Lentz!" True as those words may have been, it was disquieting in that somber moment to hear those words shouted with such exuberance.

My grandmother died as she had lived: a serene, even-tempered life. Rabbis teach that the greatest dignity to be found in death is the dignity of the life that preceded it. They often end a memorial service with the sentence, "May her memory be for a blessing." That could be said of my grandmother. Her gift to me was her quiet demeanor, her patience, her attention to me. In her 99th year she still wrote long, beautifully hand-scripted letters to me when I was in college. Her memory is indeed a blessing to me.

Unremitting grief, however, attends the death of a child who dies before coming to full bloom. When our grandson Chase died at age nineteen from a car accident, our family learned what countless others have endured: an emotional grief that can be comprehended only by those who experience it. *Grief, sorrow* are merely dictionary words until they become attached to a senseless death that matches any physical pain. There is no language for emotional pain. The comradeship of loss is a bond among those who have endured the death of a child, or the rejection of a spouse. To be left without the child to whom you have devoted your life, or the wife or husband with whom you have made a solemn vow 'til death us do part,' creates a suffering the enormity of which creates a wound that never heals. Those who have suffered such losses find some consolation in joining fellow sufferers. Acknowledging their mutual grief provides the consolation that they are not alone in the world.

We each gave a large part of ourselves to the growth and nurturing of Chase. Hearing the news from Chase's father in a morning telephone call left us gasping. Some words hit us like bullets: "Chase was killed in a car accident last night." Can the biblical promise penetrate the wall of pain created by that stark announcement?

We try to make some sense of it. So that it won't be pointless, we look for the lessons his death might teach us:

- Life or death can be determined by an act as simple as fastening a seat belt.
- Parents and grandparents are blind to the flaws of their children.
- Children follow our example
- Teenagers are not yet mentally or emotionally mature. They have the limited judgment of a teenager. They have not developed adult control of their impulses.
- Growing up today is different than it was even twenty or thirty years ago. Modern technology can be distracting. It encourages shortcuts.
- And yes, some things are beyond explanation. Few get through life without suffering a tragedy.

These lessons were taught to us with blood sacrifice. The poignant emotion and the powerful message that accompanies the death of one we love remains with us for the rest of our lifetime. It will be memorialized in ritual and recollection; first every hour, then every day, then every week. The painful spaces will widen, and the ritual will eventually become a welcome of remembrance and gratitude for what we once shared. After the shock, life continues in artificial normalcy. A thin veneer covers the pain until a particular song, a sunset, a tender story scrapes away the cover and suddenly tears are flowing. Life is never the same after enduring this kind of loss.

"It was just an accident." That is a consolation to some. A degree of respite for me came with the reflection that my grandson would never face the pronouncement, "it's terminal cancer." He would never experience the pain of rejection, the betrayal of a lover. He would miss out on life's future joys, but he would also escape the inevitable sorrows. That's the emotional mix which faces those of us who remain.

*First century philosopher Seneca wrote to a mother who was grief stricken over the death of her teenage son. He advised her to "consider that the dead are afflicted by no ills...Death is the undoing of all our sorrows...it returns us to that peace in which we reposed before we were born."*

When life and death events occur outside their natural order, there is an intuitive impulse to explain the unexplainable. Life and death are supposed to progress according to a natural order. The old pass away, the young continue on. When that order is disrupted, we construct a framework, a context that saves us from relegating life to a series of random events. Without reflection, we rush through life, avoiding the struggle of contemplation, skipping like a stone across the surface of water, until we come to the end and sink to the bottom.

What parable is contained in these life and death events? Is the story of each life predestined by a genetic code or a divine plan? There must be a deeper message, a context into which I can logically fit his nineteen years.

James Hillman, in his book *The Soul's Code: In Search of Character and Calling*[1], writes that each person's life is shaped and determined by more than genetics and environment. Each life involves an embedded theme, which is beautiful and mysterious. It is a quality that is unique to each individual; it is unmatched by any other human being, distinctive to each individual as much so as a fingerprint.

Hillman finds this uniqueness embodied in what the Greeks called the *daimon* — the core, the essence of a particular person. It is determined when each of us is born and it becomes our "calling," or "destiny." Ever since reading that book, I search for that unique *daimon* in each of my family members, and in those with whom I have the closest bond.

Is it the destiny of some to die young? Chase was a boy who relished the joy of life from the moment he arose each morning. Every day was a great adventure. One of the rewards of being a grandparent is the opportunity to see what the world looks like through the eyes of a child. We took him hiking along the slate creek river beds of Logan County, Ohio, when he was an eight-year-old. The air was cool and damp. Suddenly he cried out words of pure joy: "This is the best day of my life!" His delight at something so simple caught me by surprise. I opened my eyes to see what he was observing: the ancient trees towering over us; the sun filtering through the leaves; the deep cut of the riverbed; the smell of pure fresh air, and being together to enjoy this bountifulness of nature. It did not require the artificial entertainment of a Disney World, a midway arcade or an Xbox game. It was the unadulterated joy and satisfaction of being enveloped in the beauty of nature...together.

I risk an opinion as to what Chase's *daimonic* code might have been. After his death I spent hours thinking about his life — both waking daytime hours and sleepless nighttime hours. My collective memories led me to the conclusion that he was destined to live just nineteen years. I reached this conclusion in the best sense, with gratitude for those nineteen years, and with the calm assurance that this was his prescripted destiny. Yes, there are lessons to be learned; but there is also a destiny to accept.

He rarely if ever said "no" to an invitation to play, or to a friend who asked for help. And the response was always enthusiastic:

"Want to take a bike ride?" "Sure!"

"Will you help me plant a garden?" "Sure!"

"Would you show me how to fix my computer?" "Sure!"

When Chase was thirteen years old we scheduled a dinner at an Amish home in Ohio, where a home-cooked, family meal was prepared and served for the price of a voluntary donation. We wanted to expose Chase to the simple, spiritual life of the Amish. As we pulled into the farm lane I facetiously said to Chase, "Would you say the prayer before we are invited to sit down and eat? The Amish are very religious."

"Sure, Papa," he answered, without hesitation.

I was amazed. Was there any request from which this boy would beg off?

Chase gave of himself fully. His *daimon?* To live fully, to pack it all in, in a short period of time: Eagle Scout; track and cross country athlete; ski club; passion for music: piano, trombone, guitar; entrepreneur who came on the scene with printed business cards at the age of eight as *Owner of Mr. Snow Cone Man,* before moving on to internet trading and selling of electronics, and then launching a landscaping company when he was sixteen.

He loved working hard and fast, making money — and he made a lot of it. He loved spending money. At the mall with his friends, one of them snickered, "Chase just bought aisle nine at Home Depot." He purchased a pickup truck for his landscaping business and a BMW for his personal use.

Meanwhile, he did not stay in one place. He traveled to Australia as a ten-year-old. I took him to California, where the two of us biked in the desert and hiked in the mountains. We traveled throughout England. All of this before he was twelve years old. We traveled in Italy. He skied in Colorado.

And he worked! He loved to work and had a reputation for perfection in his landscaping business. He gave his life fully.

His *daimon?* It was to live his life quickly and fully; to get it done without wasting time. To be outdoors as much as possible and reading books as little as possible. His days were marked by velocity, haste, and agility. Sitting still and reading was dull and time wasting.

As a three-year-old, he sat on my Harley motorcycle: "Key go here. Lights go here. Gas go here, engine go *vroom, vroom*. Motorcycle go fast!" His first email address was "Speedster."

I took him to a go-cart track. He chose the go-cart in front of me. I followed, trying to catch him as he pulled farther and farther ahead. After the ride was over I asked him how he was able to keep so far ahead of me. He said, "I just pushed the accelerator down as far as it would go and never let up on it." He was ten years old.

Maybe that's what he did the night he drove his BMW around a curve in the highway. He drove so fast that the car rolled and flipped into a farmer's field. He was not wearing a seat belt. He was thrown out of the car and died instantly.

Fifteen years ago I was given a leather-bound diary as Christmas gift. I decided to interview each member of the family and write their responses in the diary. When I asked Chase, who was nine years old, to give a description of himself, he said, "My favorite foods are onions, pickles, croissants, salad, pomegranates, and pasta. I want to live in the same house with my parents for the rest of my life. I would describe myself as 'an American boy with power.'"

A girlfriend in Chase's sophomore class at Wittenberg University drove onto the campus remembering the good times they had enjoyed together, laughing… singing. There was something ominous about the questions he had shared concerning his future. Just then the song *See You Again* came on her radio. She listened to the words that took on a new meaning, wondering if he was now in a better place.

President John Adams wrote after hearing about his son's death, "A son who was once the delight of my eyes and a darling of my heart, cut off in the flower of his days… by causes which have been the greatest grief of my heart and the deepest affliction of my life…"

While reflecting on his own death, Cicero wrote, "What a wonderful day it will be when I set out to join that divine assembly of souls and leave behind this world of pain and pollution. For I shall set off to see…my own son Cato — no better or more devoted man was ever born…People think that I have born his loss bravely. No, I have felt terrible pain, but I have consoled myself that our separation would not be forever."[2]

I understand those words now. So does anyone who has lost a child.

## Grief...

We live and thrive in families, in communities. We live with and for each other. Our activities, our emotions, our thoughts are bound together. When part of our family is cut off from our existence, the pain is visceral. We lose our balance. "Happily ever after" is a fantasy that is dispelled by failure, illness, death, rejection. Each of these is a learning experience.

> *A hungry stomach, an empty wallet, a broken heart*
> *can teach you some of the best lessons in life.*
> Robin Williams

This kind of pain is instructive, possibly the most instructive, important lesson we will ever learn. Death, like rejection, can destroy us if we attempt to bury the grief associated with them. Unlike the emotions of happiness and satisfaction, grief is an oppressive emotion. We have to work with it, through it. It's exhausting. But it teaches us important information about ourselves. Buddhism teaches that we increase our suffering when we attempt to avoid it. Addictions can result from the inability to work through our grief.

Is it heroic to suppress our emotions? We probably place too much value in the stoic character. When we honor our emotions we discover that they are sources of information. When we deny our emotional suffering it becomes a cause of depression, anxiety, and surrender.

Stephen Hawking, the brilliant theoretical physicist, said, "Until I got sick I was bored with life. I drank too much. I didn't enjoy life. When I was given two years to live, I started to enjoy life. When one's expectations are reduced to zero, everything one does takes on new meaning."

Acknowledging our mortality seems like a simple thing to do. But we don't take time to consider what it means. We accuse someone of being "morbid" when he talks about his mortality, even though he may be perfectly healthy. But thoughtful reflection about the length of one's days is not the same as wallowing in despair about it. When we accept the fact that we are depressed or that we are going to die, we open the door to what this can teach us. Grief is a teacher. Fear is a teacher. These emotions teach us to become more honest with ourselves, and then to accept and love ourselves for who we are — fragile, transient creatures.

## Life After Death...

*I believe... in the resurrection of the body* (The Apostles Creed).

If this is true, what does it imply about the practice of cremation? Will there be a new, resurrected body?

Will we know each other? Will there be any recognizable qualities from our earthly existence?

Will we be reincarnated in another form of earthly life?

Will the way in which we lived our earthly life affect the quality of this resurrected existence?

Will there be a process of judgment, which will determine our fate in eternity?

Scripture does not give us definitive resolutions to these questions. Living with unknowns is part of our human condition.[3]

Speculation about an afterlife ranges from denial that it exists to an eternity of unending, hedonic gratification. The Roman philosopher Lucretius (99 B.C. — 55 B.C.) belongs to the first proposition. The author of *De Rerum Natura* (On the Nature of Things), he wrote that there is no after life and all organized religions are superstitious delusions. The goal of life, according to his philosophy, is the optimization of pleasure, by means of a disciplined hedonic calculus.

At the other end of that continuum are those who believe in the return of certain individuals as disembodied spirits, who turn lights on and off, appear in dreams, and in some cases make a visual appearance. These occurrences rely upon the willingness of an individual to accept their possibility and the ability to be receptive to them. The fact that these experiences are not universally enjoyed indicates either that some individuals are endowed with more insight or that they have a more vivid imagination.

Every religion has speculated about the possibility of existence after death, maintaining that there is some essential part of each individual's identity or spirit that continues to be known after death of the physical body. Once a religion has accepted the validity of an afterlife, the next step is to determine whether it is available to everyone, or only a select few. Universalism is the view that all individuals will ultimately be rewarded with an afterlife. Although the desire for immortality may be universal, this does not necessarily make it so. Desire is not proof. Universalism has been rejected by the majority of theologians. This leaves us with the question: might some individuals deserve eternity more than others?

Most religions anticipate a final reckoning or judgment, based on the faith and ethical behavior of the individual while alive. This harsh outcome would limit eternity to the select few individuals who have satisfied the requirements.

Christian theology takes the view that if one has faith in a God who creates human life to begin with, then one has reason to believe that this God is capable of sustaining life beyond death. Biblical scripture teaches that life beyond death is a "free gift." It is not earned by human beings living up to a certain code of conduct. If it had to be paid for in that sense, it would not be a "free gift." As T.A. Kantonen puts it, "God is not God if he is reduced to the role of spectator of human achievement."[4] This would be akin to the Jack Horner philosophy; man comes to God saying, "See what a good boy am I."

But the question of an afterlife will continue to frustrate us if we insist on certainty. For such a quest simply confronts us with the impenetrable wall of death. Everyone must die. And there is no assurance, no certainty of anything beyond death. There is only the question; will I be one of the recipients of that free gift?

"For the wages of sin is death, but the free gift of God is eternal life in Christ Jesus our Lord" (Roman 6:23). Scripture leaves no room for human justification, "for all have sinned and fallen short," so all must, as a consequence die, and await the determination of that benevolence...that gift.

If we accept the possibility of an afterlife, the next step is to consider what constitutes that life. The Islamic promise of 72 virgins awaiting the Muslim martyr may sound appealing, but it is nowhere found in the Quran. The clever myth became part of oral tradition to radicalize Muslim men and inspire them to martyrdom for the cause of jihad — the war against the enemies of Islam.

All major Indian religions (Jainism, Hinduism, Buddhism, Sikhism) believe in the idea of reincarnation, which was handed down from Greek scholars like Socrates and Plato. In the nineteenth and twentieth centuries scholars who became acquainted with Indian scriptures studied the concept of reincarnation as a psychological discipline. William James founded the "American Society for Psychical Research" in 1885. This led to the critical investigation of paranormal phenomena.

Formal Christian theology rejects reincarnation, but many Christians profess a belief in it, according to a Pew Forum survey. The Baha'i faith states that the nature of the afterlife is beyond the understanding of the living.

Research into past lives is a central tenet of the Church of Scientology. The founder of Scientology, L. Ron Hubbard, published a book about past lives entitled *Have You Lived Before This Life*. Contemporary studies by psychiatrists and psychologists have resulted in claims that evidence of a former life has emerged in certain subjects who, after being hypnotized, could speak a previously unknown foreign language. This psychic phenomenon has been labeled "xenoglossy."

According to Old Testament scriptures, all who die go to a dark place called Sheol, later named Hades. At some point judgment is rendered, separating the evil from the good. But there was an underlying conviction that life of some kind followed the death of the body. "After my skin has been destroyed (eaten by worms)," Job declared, "yet in my flesh I will see God...with my own eyes..." (Job 19:25-27).

The prophet Isaiah declared, "But your dead will live... their bodies will rise — let those who dwell in the dust wake up and shout for joy" (Isaiah 26:19).

And the Psalmist wrote "....because you will not abandon me to the realm of the dead, nor will you let your faithful one see decay" (Psalm 16:10).

In all these cases the emotions of the human heart, the wrestling of the conscience, and the intellectual search for meaning are involved in seeking an answer to our final destination. Simply believing any of these doctrines does not make them true. Healthy skepticism should always make us pause before accepting as final anyone else's belief. Truth is not determined by taking a vote. The earth was not flat during those centuries when all believed it to be so.[5] Nor did the sun revolve around the earth when the church fathers declared it as fact. Belief does not confer evidence of truth. Desire does not distinguish fact from fantasy. We must seek truth, not certainty.

## Notes

1 — Hillman, James. *The Soul's Code: In Search of Character and Calling* (New York, Random House, 1996).

2 — Cicero, *How to Grow Old: Ancient Wisdom for the Second Half of Life.* Translated by Philip Freeman (Princeton University Press, 2016) p. 173.

3 — This chapter is concluded in the chapter "The final breath."

4 — Kantonen, T.A., *Life After Death,* (Philadelphia, Fortress Press, 1962).

5 — Ibid.

# Chapter 3

# The Sacred And The Sensual

*Seeking Truth — The Beginning Of My Search...*

In the year 2015, the Evangelical Lutheran Church in America (ELCA) celebrated the 45th anniversary of women's ordination as pastors. Today there are more women graduating from Lutheran seminaries than men.

When it was proposed that women were equally qualified to be called into the Lutheran ministry, there were fearful whispers that the church would become a weakened and feminized institution. While women were becoming liberated in secular society, the church was clinging to its ancient traditions. After all didn't scripture state it unequivocally? "As in all the congregations of the saints, women should remain silent in the churches. They are not allowed to speak, but must be in submission as the law says" (1 Corinthians 14:23). Furthermore, scripture describes a God-ordained order to the home and the church: "Wives, submit to your husbands as to the Lord," and "Husbands, love your wives just as Christ loved the church" (Ephesians 5:22, 25). Until a few years ago those verses were commonly used in the marriage vows. (I wonder how many women cringed when that word "submit" was read at their wedding.)

Only men were enrolled in my graduate school theology classes, which meant that professors felt free to share a few off-color jokes without apology. But women's absence should not be understood as implying their acceptance of subordination. In fact it was always recognized that men were not only influenced by women in their decisions as husbands and fathers, but they also were capable of being manipulated like Odysseus who commanded his sailors to tie him to the mast of the ship lest he be tempted by the Sirens.

From the time of early Greek history, males prepared for battle and sexual conquest, while females worked behind the scenes, taking control by smooth-talking and artful persuasion. In the Greek comedy *Lysistrata*, by Aristophanes the women engaged in a mission to end the Peloponnesian War by denying all the men of the land any sexual privileges. They even conspired with the women of the enemy city-states to boycott their husbands as well. The play proceeded with a chorus of men attempting to sing and dance while stumbling around from persistent and painful erections.

A 1971 guide booklet with instructions for conducting a church council meeting advised the pastor to involve some of the ladies of the congregation, perhaps from the women's guild, to bring some baked cookies from home and serve coffee to the men of the church council prior to their business meeting. Today putting that policy into practice would be as imprudent as putting a condom in an offering plate.

In one way or another — either by indirection or overt influence — the magnetism of the female character has been a defining force behind almost every cultural advancement.

It was a hot October Sunday morning and underneath the cassock and surplice I could feel the sweat trickling down my chest, soaking the black clerical shirt. This was not an ordinary Sunday. It was the day I was to administer the sacrament of Holy Communion for the first time as an ordained 26-year-old Lutheran minister.

The liturgical prelude for this event is intense and spiritual. I turned to the altar where, thankfully, no one could see my flushed face, the beads of sweat on my brow. I read the appropriate preface:

*It is indeed right and salutary that we should at all times and in all places give thanks unto you, O Lord, Holy Father, Almighty, Everlasting God...*

I felt light-headed and nervous as the pipe organ intervened to lead the congregational response:

*Holy, holy, holy, Lord God of power and might; heaven and earth are full of your glory; Hosanna in the highest. Blessed is he who comes in the name of the Lord.*

Could I continue without thinking of how we celebrated a communion of a different sort last night?

*Holy art thou, Almighty and merciful God. Holy art thou, and great is the majesty of thy glory.*

— Let's snuggle.

— You know what that leads to.

— It's okay.

— But I have to get up early in the morning.

— I'll make sure you get up on time.

*And unto thee, O God, Father, Son, and Holy Spirit, be all honor and glory in thy holy church, world without end. Amen.*

Concentrate on what you're doing. Shut out the distractions and maintain a pious focus:

*Our Lord Jesus Christ, in the night in which he was betrayed took bread...*

Thank you, Lord. I am an earthen vessel, cracked and faulty. Use me, your imperfect servant, for the spiritual benefit of the faithful people in this congregation.

*The more pious you are, the more dangerous you are.*
Richard Rohr

I watched attentively, assuming my most spiritual demeanor, as the usher directed the first table of communicants to the altar. Again my piety withered as the one at the head of the line appeared in a mini-skirt and a far more revealing blouse than one would expect from a young lady approaching the altar with such a chaste attitude. She held her palms together devoutly, pointing heavenward above her more than ample bosom. I judiciously focused my gaze on her left ear as I handed her the "Body of Christ."

Thomas Moore said, "Traditional religion elevates the pious, other worldly individuals, then acts surprised when we discover they are interested in money and sex."

✠ ✠ ✠

Courses in theology did not prepare me for the mundane tasks of parish ministry. On my first day in the church office, I stopped to say hello to the church secretary, Mary Mook.

Having filled this position for forty years, she assumed a strong sense of ownership of every detail of the church's ministry. And so with the authority that accompanied her seniority she informed me that I should go and organize all the Sunday school books, dividing them by subject and age group.

I was prepared to answer probing questions about life after death, the efficacy of prayer, even Kierkegaard's doctrine of the teleological suspension of the ethical. Obediently, I spent the next several hours straightening out a vast library of books that were in a state of total disarray.

*When the ego dies, the soul awakes.* Gandhi

After I became known as "pastor," or "reverend," I faced challenges for which theological instruction had not prepared me. Just as many patients expect their doctor to heal their bodies miraculously, even after a lifetime of abuse, so too some expect the minister to come up with the right words to create miraculous changes: to create purpose in a person's life, and make depression disappear; to convince a wife to return to her forsaken husband; even to reverse the grisly outgrowth of cancer in a dying child.

I discovered that one of the most difficult challenges of ministry was to forfeit the claim of having all the answers regarding right and wrong, evil and good. Often only paradox exists where certainty is sought. Most of us admire and want to follow the leader who exudes confidence and clear direction. But the complexity of the human spiritual condition defies infallibility. Spiritual certainty leads to a judgmental, self-righteous nature.

Gregory Corrigan in his book *Disciple Story: Every Christian's Journey*[1] wrote this story: A rabbi was asked to adjudicate a dispute between two men. The first man presented his argument, and the rabbi, after hearing his evidence said to him, "You are right!" Then the second man presented his argument and the rabbi, after hearing his evidence, said, "You are right!" At this point, the rabbi's wife turned to her husband and asked, "How can both of these men be right?" The rabbi thought for a moment and then said, "Darling, you are right!"

It's a humorous story with a poignant lesson. "Truth is rarely pure and never simple." Certitude is inflexible. Skepticism leaves the mind open for new evidence, and the spirit receptive to more reformation. Intransigence leads to argumentation, bickering, and divorce.

Bertrand Russell put it this way: The whole problem with the world is that "the stupid are cocksure, while the intelligent are full of doubt."

## Notes

1 — Corrigan, Gregory, *Disciples Story: Every Christian's Journey*. Notre Dame, IN.; Ave Maria Press, 1989, p.93.

# Chapter 4

# Cry At The Birth...
# Rejoice At The Death

*Per aspera ad astra...*

Thirteenth-century priest Thomas Aquinas said, "No one can live without joy." But what is it that brings joy to our lives? A Harvard study that took place over the past eighty years asked Americans to report the source of their own happiness. It is the longest study ever conducted. They found that happiness was not related to money or fame. It was independent of physical appearance or possessions. Those who rated their happiness at the highest level were individuals with close, enduring relationships. It was not the number of relationships, but the quality of a few important connections that produced the most joy in life. That single factor determined not only the level of happiness, but also longevity, and even physical comfort. Those who were unhappy in their eighties felt more pain in older age.

The marriages which endured into old age, according to the study, were not those in which the partners simply felt satisfied. Rather it was those that continued growing in richness, understanding, and sensitivity, maturing together, changing and shaping one another's habits, forming new goals together, and finding common purpose.

Intimacy was also shown to be important to human health and happiness. Lack of human touch is not only disappointing, it is painful. Physical touching releases oxytocin. It reduces pain; it increases cognitive ability, including math skills. Scientific tests show that it can reduce the effect of electric shock.

*The supreme human experience is to share a thought and then to touch.*

When asked, most people, especially young people, said they believed that money and recognition were the most important ingredients for a secure and happy life. Of those aged 22-37, 80% claimed that their life goal was to be rich.

An observant skeptic soon realizes just how unrelated wealth and happiness can be. It was illustrated by French photographer Henri Cartier-Bresson, who was a master of candid photography. He often spotted and photographed scenes of apparent contradictions. Steve Goodier described one of Cartier-Bresson's famous photographs taken in a poor section of Seville, Spain. (This story is taken from Steve Goodier's blog: *http://www.LifeSupportSystem.com.*)

The photography shows a run-down alley surrounded by crumbling walls and riddled with bullet holes. The setting elicits feelings of sadness. But then you see the contradiction: within that drab setting children are playing. They wear dirty and torn clothing, but there is laughter on their faces and the expression of carefree joy. In the foreground a small boy on crutches hobbles away from two other boys, his face lit up with a broad grin. One boy is laughing so hard he has to hold his side. Others lean on the cracked walls, beaming with delight.

The picture is instructive. Happiness is found among those with whom we can laugh and play. It depends not on external circumstances or prosperity, but an internal connection and understanding with a friend. Apparently it is a goal for which many are seeking. Yale University instituted a course called Happiness 101. The class has the highest enrollment of any that the University offers, and is over-subscribed each semester. (More on this subject at the end of this chapter.)

Money makes a difference, but not what most think. It has diminishing returns. The more we have of it, the more the joy factor wears off. The level of happiness gradually increases up to an annual salary of $75,000, but above that, there is not much increase in security or satisfaction.

The paradox of money is that while earning more may give a temporary uplift, we actually become happier by giving it away than by spending it on ourselves. The satisfaction of finding just the right gift for a favorite person brings more delight than receiving a present.

Happiness also increases when we discipline our desires. In a famous experiment, which is now well known, researchers offer a marshmallow to four-year-olds. Each child is brought into a room and given a single marshmallow. He is told he can eat it, but if he waits five minutes until the researcher returns, he will be given an additional marshmallow to eat. The child can eat it right away or save it. "It's up to you," the researcher says.

The children were tracked for many years afterward. The primary finding was that the kids who exercised self-restraint and did *not* eat the marshmallow were happier and more confident. They had more friends, got better grades and ultimately had better jobs. The key was the ability to delay self-gratification.

The tradition of Lent has advocated the practice of forty days of abstinence from pleasure as a spiritual discipline. In times past it involved penitence; in recent years it has taken on a more secular discipline as a time to break an addiction or lose weight. Ramadan, the ninth month of the Muslim lunar calendar is likewise a time during which devout Muslims are penitent and fast from sunrise to sunset.

Muslims world-wide observe this tradition, which requires abstention from food and water from sunrise to sunset. During the long days of May that means a fourteen-hour fast. Sabeeha Rehman describes the spiritual exercise: "The first few days are trying. I miss my morning coffee, my afternoon fruit snack...Yet by the time Ramadan is over, I instinctively pull back my hand when offered a pastry or samosa. My clothes fit better and my blood-sugar level is great. I find it easier to say the five daily prayers consistently...My husband is not fasting, which makes for a lonely pre-dawn meal for me. He is under treatment for cancer and has to take his medication and stay hydrated.

The sick, as well as pregnant or breast-feeding women, are exempt from fasting. But they are obligated either to make up for the missed fast at a later date or feed the poor for each day of missed fast."

Ms. Rehman says that this observance of Ramadan is especially instructive for the young. It teaches them self-restraint and the habit of "deflecting aggression." She expresses gratitude for America's principle of religious tolerance, a doctrine established by the founding fathers after coming here to escape religious persecution. A school in Michigan allows Muslim students to attend gym practice at night. At Haverford College the cafeteria provided a 4 a.m. boxed breakfast every day. "These simple acts of kindness and accommodation reaffirmed my faith in the American value of religious freedom."[1]

In the 1950s public schools made it a practice to avoid scheduling meetings or athletic events on Wednesday nights in order to accommodate Lenten midweek prayer services. Most entertainment activities were cancelled during Lent. Blue Laws, also known as Sunday laws, banned commercial activities on Sunday, so stores were closed. Most blue laws have been repealed in the United States. Until February 28, 2018, Indiana continued to ban the sale of alcoholic beverages on Sundays, and many states ban the sale of cars on Sundays. Growing up with the assumption that shopping was not available on Sunday, it still seems strange to me as an adult to realize that I can buy groceries or go to a hardware store on Sunday, just as any other day.

Religion, or at least some spiritual outlet or form of expression, has been shown to be a factor in overall happiness. Counselors for the depressed advise setting aside a time each day to make a list of good things that have happened to them. They advise keeping a daily journal, even calling one person each day to express gratitude for their friendship. In earlier days it was called "counting your blessings."

Age plays a role in surveys on happiness. At age eighteen it peaks, but then declines until we reach the fifties. Depression is the most prominent between ages 38 and 44, according to Andrew Shatte, professor of psychology at University of Arizona.[2]

As we move into the fifties, hormones become more manageable, competitive instincts become more controllable, and happiness rises even higher than it was at age eighteen; we choose to spend our time with quality relationships; we become more discerning and these relationships are what nourish our sense of well-being. Being with happy, optimistic people who laugh, who see the glass as half full, enhances our satisfaction and happiness.

Marc Agronin, professor at University of Miami, warns that there is a potential downside to aging.[3] Mental deterioration is a normal process of getting old. A moderate decline occurs in our seventies and more severe decline happens in our eighties. These conditions can be made worse by hearing and vision loss, and even more so by alcohol, stress, depression, and poor sleep. Cicero said, "Growing old is a matter of character, not of age. Those who are mean-spirited and irritable will be unhappy at every period of their lives."

The good news is that not everything declines as we grow old. Some things get better. Aging provides us with the free time to become more creative. Many artists have reached their peak creating some of their best works late in age. Henri Matisse did not allow a stroke to stop him. He created artistic paper cut-outs after he could no longer practice his skill with the paint brush. Thomas Edison produced the telephone at age 84. David Trumble of Canada published his first book at age 109 and danced with a partner at 114. "Old men ought to be explorers," T.S. Eliot said. "They should be less hesitant to speak their mind, to risk failure, to face rejection."

I have found it less daunting to speak to a stranger, and coming from an older man it is less threatening when I approach another person. I don't have to suppress my curiosity. I can pursue the risky venture of asking invasive questions. Acting appropriately is not so necessary. Exploring the world of ideas and the eccentricities of human behavior can be as exciting as physical pleasures. "A thought is a tremendous mode of excitement," Alfred North Whitehead wrote.

I resist falling into that category of the "elderly" although I may appear that way to others.

*Often the soul ripens into fuller goodness even as age spreads its ugly film so that mere glances do not divine the preciousness of the fruit.*[4]

The key to maintaining a healthy brain is preserving a positive attitude. We can become more critical as we age. Cranky old people are no fun to be around and are soon avoided. And in the absence of healthy mental stimulation we start to worry, and fall into the habit of anticipating the worst possible outcome. I agree with Mark Twain when he said, "There have been many catastrophes in my life, some of which really happened."

'Thinking young' helps us stay young. Agronin advises people to exercise, observe good diet (avoid binge eating) and cross-train the brain (learn something new or do something different.) Get involved in a good cause.

Marc Agronin tells about one of his patients, an active 106-year-old lady who campaigns for people to get out and vote. She is also involved in her son's love life. Her 84-year-old son doesn't always appreciate the advice from his 106-year-old mother.

Does where you live make a difference to your happiness and well-being? Not necessarily. But there is the story of the doctor who told his patient he had six months to live.

The reply was, "Oh no, what I can I do?" The doctor said for him to go to North Dakota. "Will I live longer that way?" he asked. "No, but it will feel like forever."

It's a humorous story, but studies have been conducted to determine where people were the happiest based on several factors: work environment, emotional and physical well-being, and community support. The states which measured the highest in test studies were Minnesota, Utah, and Hawaii. The lowest ranked were Louisiana, Oklahoma, and West Virginia.

The story is told in Greek literature about the wise sage and philosopher, Solon, who was invited to visit Croesus, the ancient king of Lydia. The king greeted him warmly and for several days put on a display of his wealth to illustrate how fortunate he was. Then Croesus said to Solon, "My Athenian friend, I have heard about your wisdom and knowledge. Who is the happiest man you have ever seen?" King Croesus waited expectantly to hear his name. But flattery was not part of Solon's character. He proceeded to describe the lives of three individual men, each of whom was dead. King Croesus was livid. They were three dead individuals of no distinction, all supposedly superior in good fortune to him. Was he not happier than those peons? But Solon explained that although the rich have advantages, such as "the means to bear calamity and satisfy their appetites," they have no monopoly on the things that are truly valuable in life: healthy children, sufficient nourishment, a sound body." Granted the king had more money, but riches can create problems; the more money, the more complications. Life is uncertain, Solon explained. While you may be enjoying power and riches today, you have no idea what calamity might be in store for you tomorrow. Whether or not your life can be described as "happy" can't be determined until the moment of your death. "Count no man happy until he is dead," Solon advised.

Solon's admonition proved to be prophetic. Croesus' beloved son died soon after in a hunting accident, and in a battle with Persia, Croesus was captured and placed in chains on top of a giant funeral pyre. As he died with the flames licking his feet, Croesus cried out, "Oh Solon! Oh Solon! Count no man happy until he is dead!"[5]

✢ ✢ ✢

Most of us do not welcome the prospect of our own death, regardless of what promise there is of an afterlife. But comfort and security in this earthly life are distributed inequitably. Celebration normally accompanies the birth of a child. That's not necessarily the case with all classes of society. The early slaves in our country lamented, "Cry at the birth; rejoice at the death." They were acknowledging that every child brought into the world would endure a life of servitude and suffering. Some pregnancies across all social classes are unwelcome. Many marriages are resigned to a loveless co-existence. The happiness quotient is unevenly distributed.

But happy or not, is human life, the crowning gem of evolution, brought into existence only for a destiny of mere extinction? There is within the genetic code of humanity an intuitive perception that life is more than that which we experience in the here and now. It is expressed in the creed which I grew up reciting every Sunday: "I believe in the communion of saints, the forgiveness of sins...the life everlasting."

Other religions may express it differently, but for those who plumb the depths of life's spiritual meaning, it comes to the same thing: surely we are not meant for extinction. That is the only thing which makes death in any way acceptable; otherwise the creation of a newborn life in many parts of the world is a sadistic joke.

Regardless of when a person dies, at whatever age, young or old, grief endures for those left behind. And the anticipation of our own demise can be depressing. I ponder the fact that my life will end, and I grow more cautious as my remaining days diminish, unlike my younger years when I was brash and took reckless chances, feeling as though I was invulnerable. I find it strange to imagine that I will someday no longer exist. And yet nature has a way of softening the apprehension. As my body gets weaker, as I develop more pains, as I sleep less soundly and become tired more quickly, I begin to welcome the thought that it will someday end. But, still, I ponder the thought that I will never again taste that tiramisu or *Coq au Vin*; nevermore enjoy the warmth of an embrace; never feel the sand on my feet; never in this life.

The Yale University course "Psychology and the Good Life," is available free of charge online if you sign up at coursera.com. Before doing that, you may wish to take the "Authentic Happiness Inventory" offered by the University of Pennsylvania. The quiz is also available online. I scored 3.15 on a 5 point scale.

The four months of Yale lectures have become wildly popular. Many college students today are unhappy and depressed. One administrator of a small liberal arts college told me that they have two full time counselors on staff who do nothing but counsel students suffering from stress and depression.

The second lecture in this Yale series informs students that about fifty percent of happiness is determined by genetic influence; forty percent can be controlled by your thoughts and attitudes. The most reliable sources of happiness are family and friends, being physically active, and developing a disciplined sense of gratitude and optimism.[6]

A skeptic says, "I may be happy, but I won't know for certain until I share it with others."

## Notes

1 — Rehman, Sabeeha, "How America Makes Ramadan Easier," published in the Wall Street Journal *Houses of Worship* column, Friday, June 1, 2018.

2 — Andrew Shatte, Ph.D. presented a paper at the One Day University, November 23, 2014 in St. Petersburg, Florida. He is the co-author with Karen Reivich, Ph.D. of *The Resilience Factor: 7 Keys to Finding Your Inner Strength and Overcoming Life's Hurdles, (New York,* Broadway Books, 2002).

3 — Agronin, Marc E., M.D. *A Doctor's Journey into the Heart of Growing Old,* DaCapo Lifelong Books, 2011
Marc Agronin delivered a lecture on the subject *How the Brain Ages: What We Know Now,* at "One Day University" in St. Petersburg, Florida on November 23, 2014.

4 — Eliot, George, *Silas Marner,* (Orland, Maine, Ginn and Company, 1927).

5 — Arkenberg, J.S., Dept. of History, Cal State Fullerton. May have modernized the text. Ancient History Sourcebook: Solon & Croesus. [https://sourcebooks.fordham.edu]

6 — The article, "How to be happier," was printed in *The Week* magazine, August 17/August 24, 2018 issue. The review was excerpted from an essay that originally appeared in *New York* magazine.

# Chapter 5

# Seeking Truth...

*Believe the one who seeks the truth. Doubt the one who finds it.*
    Andre Gide

I do not claim that the search for truth will ever result in the discovery of a foundation of certainty. Nor is that the objective. Seeking truth is an ongoing process. As we mature we learn that it is necessary to integrate new information. Otherwise, our rationality can become as irrelevant as those who continue to claim that the world was flat. Such a person today is the Luddite with a technophobic propensity.

Philosopher Charles Pierce explains that truth "is not standing upon the bedrock of fact. It is walking upon a bog, and can only say, this ground seems to hold for the present. Here I will stay until it begins to give way."1 We engage in self-deception when we convince ourselves that the judgments we bring to life's moments are the same as assertions of certainty.

Embracing skepticism requires discipline and humility. When confronted with conflicting information it intrudes with the warning, "you might be wrong." Skepticism strengthens our ability to sort cautiously through the multitude of conflicting sources of information that assault us, as well as the unfounded claims on social media that leave us all scratching our heads. Skepticism encourages us to be curious. It advises us to ask more questions.

Certitude, as opposed to skepticism, retards our capacity to examine new information, or information that is inconsistent with our assumptions. It leads to a stale and stagnant personality. The cure? Be curious. Ask questions. Explore human nature. Resist conjuring negative judgments against anyone who doesn't see it your way.

*Judge a man by his questions rather than his answers.*
Voltaire

✠ ✠ ✠

During the break from a meeting with business and academic leaders, a man I had just met asked me, "What do you find to be the most meaningful Bible passage?" I wondered what prompted the question. Normally the next comment after 'nice to meet you' is 'where are you from?' Was he testing me? Was he experiencing a personal trauma? He didn't know my background, so the question seemed odd, but more creative than "What do you do for a living?" It was simply out of character in the setting of that business conference.

James Fallows and Deborah Fallows have written in the book *Our Town* that the 'second question' asked after an introduction reveals something about the character of the participants. In New York, that question might be, 'what do you do?' An introduction taking place in a small southern town might be followed by, 'where do you go to church?'

I assumed that the question from this New Jersey fellow implied that if I was a moderately literate individual, I should be acquainted with the content of this Holy Writ, which at one time was the most prominent writing in the English language — and today perhaps one of the most ignored.[2] I might have answered the question with the first thing that came to my mind — maybe a reference to the Sermon on the Mount, or Psalm 23. Although my personal faith is qualified with suspended judgment, I recognize the significance that religion has had in my life and the lives of millions. It has played a decisive role in our culture and even our language.

For centuries, after the invention of the printing press, the Bible was the most prominent book in Western culture. Idiomatic expressions from the Bible continue to be part of our daily conversation:

The blind leading the blind…
By the skin of your teeth…
A leopard can't change his spots…
Eat, drink, and be merry…
Cast the first stone…
Fly in the ointment…
Go the extra mile…

And that's just a "drop in the bucket," another phrase from the Bible (Isaiah 40:15).

I answered that it was probably Psalm 23, but having had more time to reflect on what specific verses of biblical literature have most impacted my thinking, I would respond with a reference to Romans 8:38-39.[3]

These two verses in Paul's letter to the Romans, proclaiming an indestructible source of love, project a stubborn optimism that there is a positive dimension to life, and a purposeful reason for human existence. Despite colossal tragedy — war, famine, earthquakes, cancer, mass murders, floods, untimely deaths of children, ravaging forest fires, and man's inhumanity to man — these verses testify that somehow, either in this life or another, goodness and mercy may rise from the ashes of human degradation to reveal the intention of a benevolent Power that set the universe into motion. While suffering is an inescapable part of human experience, these verses espouse a teleological resolution that prohibits human existence from being an absurd twist of meaningless fate.

It would be gratifying if spiritual life transpired according to absolutes; for example, if we could accept in faith that the content of the Bible is infallible, despite the contradictions and distortions which it contains. Reason prohibits such naïve assumptions. The paradox of religious faith is to be committed, yet also aware that we could be wrong. It is the dialectic relationship between conviction and doubt. It takes more courage to let go of certitude, to accept the possible error of our beliefs, than to ignore or defy any judgment that does not coincide with our own.

The mission statement of Carthage College in Kenosha, Wisconsin is "Seeking Truth, Building Strength, Inspiring Service...Together." The statement emerged from a committee which I chaired, and was condensed from our multiple committee discussion sessions by the creative wordsmith Robert Rosen. "Seeking truth" jumps out as soon as we start to question a statement that does not tally with our own view. Faith gives us the courage to forge ahead, always testing, always challenging our focus to deepen our insight, when it does not correspond with others. Einstein said, "Condemnation without examination is the height of ignorance."

My father sheepishly confessed to me that his own father, an attorney who became a Lutheran minister, had once said to him, "Don't trust anyone, even your own brother." A cynical statement, but perhaps realistic in its recognition of human imperfection. As we advance from childhood into adolescence we begin to ask more questions. We come to realize that some of the things we learned in science classes disputed our immature assumptions, at times even the claims of our parents. Recently we have been warned about trusting social media. As a teenager I read the hyperbolic proverb encouraging skepticism: "Believe half of what you see and nothing of what you hear," a statement credited to Edgar Allan Poe.

In the novel *A Soldier of the Great War*, two characters discuss the differences in their core beliefs, one a Marxist and the other a Christian. The Christian explains that his belief is not an organized system, but an "overwhelming combination of all that I've seen, felt, and cannot explain, that has stayed with me and of which I am not sure, that is alluring because it will not stoop to be defined by so inadequate a creature as man. Unlike Marxism, it is ineffable, and it cannot be explained in words."[4] As soon as we use words to define faith we begin to humanize it, limit its potential.

Humanity has come a long way in evolutionary development, but is still characterized by treachery and betrayal.

We make commitments — marital and financial — in faith, if not in expectation — trusting that our faith is well placed. And because of human frailty, we find that there is no ultimate security in human relationships. We reach higher, to the representation of an absolute. For many it is found in the New Testament scripture: "Don't be deceived…every good and perfect gift is from above, coming down from the Father of the heavenly lights, who does not change like shifting shadows" (James 1:17). The hymn that is sung in some churches, *Abide with Me*, contains the verse, "Change and decay in all around I see, O thou who changest not, abide with me."

Even at this point, prudence would advise that we continue "Seeking Truth"; for as long as we exist in this earthbound form, our knowledge is limited. New Testament scripture itself warns us not to be too certain, for "now we see but a poor reflection as in a mirror…" (1 Corinthians 13:12).

We may continue to challenge, yet be guided by the tenants of faith, because they provide a framework from which we can attempt to interpret the meaning of our existence and our responsibility to others. Even if we engage in the spiritual practices of prayer, worship, and study of biblical literature, we must hold in reserve an opening for questions, so that in "seeking truth" we leave room to expand our understanding of reality. We know that we will inevitably bump up against others whose "truth" is not defined in the same way as ours.

History is replete with evidence of conflict, tragedy, and human bloodshed that can result from the war of words over conflicting religious and political convictions. Political divisions have grown so deep that fist fights break out in unlikely places. A public exercise gym had to remove their television from the facility after a fight ensued between two weight lifters watching Fox news.

Those who claim that their beliefs, whether religious or political, are infallible become malicious and subversive.

Friedrich Nietzsche said, "Convictions are more danger-ous enemies of truth than lies." Wise individuals respond to opposing views with equanimity. They leave room for questions. Faith and doubt are not antithetical. The history of intelligent leadership in every field of endeavor gives us examples.

Lincoln privately admitted his doubts about human equality, while openly preserving his commitment to end slavery and unify the country. The archbishop of Canter-bury admitted that at times he questioned if God was there. Martin Luther struggled to the point of despair over his doubts. John Calvin, another prominent figure in the Prot-estant Reformation, acknowledged moments of uncertainty. Mother Teresa wrote in her diaries, published posthumous-ly, that there were moments of "terrible darkness" within her. The psalmist cried out, "You have taken from me my closest friends and have made me repulsive to them...Why, O Lord, do you reject me and hide your face from me?" (Psalm 88), Those who build a wall around their creed de-prive themselves of new insights. When we have the cour-age to admit our doubts, we open our minds to a wider in-tellectual universe. Commitment is most robust not when it is without doubt, but when it is in spite of doubt.

*There lives more faith in honest doubt, believe me,*
*than in half the creeds.*
Alfred Lord Tennyson

One of the most eloquent expressions of commitment, despite self-doubt, was written by German pastor and theo-logian Dietrich Bonhoeffer while he was in prison, shortly before his execution by the Nazis. In this poem, Bonhoeffer reveals his human vulnerability, his doubts about his iden-tity.

## Who Am I?

Dietrich Bonhoeffer (March 4, 1945)[5]
Who am I? They often tell me
I would step from my cell's confinement
calmly, cheerfully, firmly,
like a squire from his country-house.
Who am I? They often tell me
I would talk to my warders
freely and friendly and clearly,
as though it were mine to command.

Who am I? They also tell me
I would bear the days of misfortune
equably, smilingly, proudly,
like one accustomed to win.

Am I then really all that which other men tell of?
Or am I only what I know of myself,
restless and longing and sick, like a bird in a cage,
struggling for breath, as though hands were
compressing my throat,
yearning for colors, for flowers, for the voices of birds,
thirsting for words of kindness, for neighborliness,
trembling in expectation of great events,
powerlessly trembling for friends at an infinite distance,
weary and empty at praying, at thinking, at making,
faint, and ready to say farewell to it all?

Who am I? This or the other?
Am I one person today, and tomorrow another?
Am I both at once? A hypocrite before others,
and before myself a contemptibly woebegone weakling?

Or is something within me still like a beaten army,
fleeing in disorder from victory already achieved?
Who am I? They mock me, these lonely questions of
mine.
Whoever I am, Thou knowest, O God, I am Thine.

## Notes

1 — This quotation was used in the book *On Truth,* by Simon
Blackburn. It was quoted in a review of the book by Julian Bag-
gini, printed in the Wall Street Journal, 7/25/2018 edition.

2 — "The Bible's influence has been all pervasive ever since
the printing press made it widely available....It is now properly remarked that for probably the first time in the history of
recent Western culture, the Bible is not at all widely studied...
there is a growing ignorance of its nature and all-pervading influence on common areas of life and literature." R. John Elford,
*The Ethics of Uncertainty: A New Christian Approach to Moral De-
cision Making, p. 71-72.(Boston, One World Publications, 2000).

3 — *For I am convinced that neither death nor life, neither angels
nor demons, neither the present nor the future, nor any powers, neither height nor depth, nor anything else in all creation, will be able
to separate us from the love of God that is in Christ Jesus our Lord.*
Romans 8:38-39 NIV Bible

4 — Helprin, Mark. *A Soldier of the Great War.* (New York, Har-
court Brace Jovanovich, 1991.

5 — Bonhoeffer, Dietrich, "Who Am I?." *Letters and Papers from
Prison,* (New York, Touchstone, 1953/1997.

# Chapter 6

# What The World Needs Now...

*Criticism is one of the lowest forms of communication.*

I welcome the portrayal of a universe at the center of which is a universal sovereign who has an unconditional love for every individual. I make no unqualified claims about the existence, form or substantiality of this supreme being, but I can conceive of no advantage that might result from insisting that there must be hard and fast tangible evidence. Skepticism allows for questions and searching. Absolute denial insinuates arrogance. It assumes the capacity to comprehend not only all that exists within the realm of physical reality, but cosmic and metaphysical as well. "A God comprehended is no God, and the theology that pretends to know everything is a sham." (John Chrysostom, Archbishop of Constantinople, 349 AD)

Maybe a theologian's job is not to prove that God exists, but to pose the right questions about life. A spiritual leader should help people work through life's complexities and face uncertainties.

When, during a chance encounter, it becomes known to some folks that I have a background as a clergyman, they become more open and communicative (after apologizing for their *French.*) They confess sensitive details about their lives. They are a bit more human and authentic. It's as though a door opens in their mind, "Maybe this is someone I can trust; someone I don't have to impress."

Worship is sought by some as a refuge from the ambiguity and stress of existence. It is a solace to the insecure that fear failure, a balm to those who are ill, or face a difficult decision. The desire for definitive answers from an authority that speaks with conviction and delivers unquestioning certainty provides a respite from nagging doubt and uncertainty. But dogmatic authorities can also misguide and deceive us. Pompous preachers proclaim what will make them popular. Beware of naiveté when your assumptions are no longer being challenged; when you are being told only what you want to hear. We should be more trusting of one who asks new questions, who challenges our lethargy, not one who presumes to have all the answers.

When in past years I was preaching every Sunday, I received compliments after the service if I had spoken about miracles and healing. When I preached about what Jesus preached — pray for those who persecute you, avoid the accumulation of wealth, stop worrying about tomorrow — the response was less receptive. Blessed are the merciful!? Practice humility!? Don't judge others!? After that kind of sermon, folks slipped out quietly to get home for Sunday dinner.

During my senior year in college I read a book which caused me to be wary of the hypocrisy of corporate worship. The book was entitled *Black Like Me,* by John Howard Griffin.[1] As an experiment, Griffin, a white man, traveled throughout the south in the 1950s, worshiping in a different church every Sunday. At each church he was warmly welcomed as a guest by the minister and members of the congregation.

Then he returned home and over a period of several months went through a chemical process which darkened the color of his skin. He enhanced the transformation with make-up techniques that gave him the appearance of an African American. After completing this transformation, he returned — unrecognized — to each of those same churches he had visited months earlier. He was stunned at how differently he was treated. Deacons of the congregations, pious, sophisticated church ladies, some of whom had previously invited him to their homes for Sunday dinner, now refused to sit near him. In some churches it was questionable whether they would even permit him to worship with them. The experience proved how irrational people can be, determining the value of a human life simply by the physical appearance of skin color. Their prejudice was an impenetrable barrier to the practice of a Christian ethic. It gave validity to the statement that Sunday morning worship is the most segregated, anti-Christian hour in America. I began to wonder if church membership was like any other human organization: simply the opportunity for like-minded people to gather and confirm their mutual biases, instead of an opportunity to confess their weaknesses, to humble themselves, to be instructed, to share compassionately with others of all description and color.

I try to imagine respectful, white church women's reaction if a black president were to publicly refer to his daughter as a "piece of ass." Or what they would say if a black president were to boast about his sexual prowess with women: "When you're a star, they let you do it." But we already know how white church ladies would react if a black president said those things. And we also know how they respond when a former reality television actor, now president, makes those remarks. It's okay…for no other reason than that he is white. No skepticism from those ladies. Just grin and bear it, Melania. ("But don't let me catch my husband doing it!")

It isn't only the injustice of biased judgment that blurs our vision. More egregious than judging by two different standards, depending on skin color, is the apparent inability or unwillingness to evaluate presidential leadership capacity by consistent standards.

Surveys taken in 2015 and 2016, before the November presidential election, indicated the qualities most desired in a president. When asked for one characteristic, the words most often mentioned were "honesty," "intelligence," "integrity." Today none of those words are used to describe the president; perhaps because they don't exist.

In 2015 citizens expressed concern about the political polarization, saying they wanted a president who would unite our country; a leader who would set a high standard of behavior for himself or herself and the government. Surveys revealed that people wanted a president whose speech reflected respect for all Americans, as well as a strong foreign policy leader who conveyed our American ideals across the globe on human rights, democracy, and tolerance. He or she should be a president who shows compassion for political adversaries, putting country ahead of party, no matter what the consequences. People in 2015 said they were tired of the political polarization. Citizens mentioned the importance of Constitutional knowledge and a strong intellect, like Angela Merkel, Chancellor of Germany who has a Ph.D. in physical chemistry. Remember, these were the ideals most highly prized by Americans in the eighteen months before the election of our current president.

When I talk to some of the same people today, they don't mention those qualities. I ask what they think about morality, importance of allies, and security; they say that those issues are not as important as taxes and jobs. Money is more important than morality.

The opening verses of the Bible create a reality drama that places the onus of this problem on the flawed human tendency to be pernicious and petty. Even if we had all been created one size and color, our belligerent human nature would have discovered ways to divide into pre-determined classes — some superior to others. We form tribal identities, creating artificial divisions according to ethnic differences, physical appearance, or degree of wealth, education, or achievement. We claim superiority over those with less, and we conceal a thin veil of resentment toward those with more.

It's not just skin color that affects how we assess the worth or value of a person. Public school teachers can be influenced by their untested assumptions of which students are the brightest and most trustworthy.

In the 1940s a small group of boys from neighboring farms got together and terrorized the neighborhoods of a city in Illinois. They raped young girls and committed several murders. From then on a cloud of suspicion hung over every young farm kid. Prejudice against boys in bib overalls spread through small towns outside the area. Paranoia was triggered as much by a boy's farm background as by a dark skin color or Muslim head covering. Many of those who lived through that period are more sensitive today to prejudice and bigotry against African Americans. They say, "We know what that feels like!"

During that period a young boy from a one-room country school moved into the town where I lived. He began attending our eighth grade class. His former school had consisted of twelve students in seven grades, all taught by one teacher. His father had been killed in a farm accident. The boy's mother was unable to care for all her children alone, so she moved the boy into town with his grandmother.

Our teacher, who had transferred to our school from a large city, considered herself to be more informed and sophisticated than others in our community. Because of the previous incident involving violent young farm boys, she held a negative bias against our new classmate. She distrusted the boy and showed disdain toward his questions. Because he was a farm boy, she did not see him as an individual, but as a potential threat, someone who belonged to a potentially dangerous class of people. Her faulty judgment was the same as those who classify all Muslims or all African Americans as inferior or dangerous. Her bias was transparent as she spent less time explaining answers to his questions (he had many) or supporting his academic efforts. She was shocked when the results of a standardized achievement test came out at the end of the school year. He scored not only at the top of our class, but one of the highest test scores the school had seen. She had not been smart enough to question her own illegitimate judgment.

A teacher is likely to give more attention to a student she assumes is a better learner. Classroom monitoring has revealed that inexperienced teachers will spend less time with those students they assume are not as bright, who are introverted or backward. They devote more time to the others, answering questions in more detail, explaining information more patiently.

Misjudgment and prejudice are caused by irrational assumptions. Bigotry can be triggered by a different religion, language, national origin, even physical characteristics. Individuals who are overweight or obese have confided suffering the effects of prejudice. Hiring practice in business shows a preference for tall men. In the professional world a man in the top quarter percentile of height is associated with an increase in salary of fifteen percent. Each inch of height adds almost $800 a year in elevated earnings in the job market, which amounts to thousands of dollars over a lifetime. Thomas Gregor, an anthropologist at Vanderbilt University, studied cultures in various parts of the world, and reported that in no case did he ever find a preference for short men.

Consider how this raises the importance of skepticism. It motivates us to look more deeply, to make more intelligent judgments about individuals, avoiding the shallow presumptions that mode of dress, height, weight, skin color, or physical morphology have any relationship to intelligence or human value.

We are not far removed from the cruelty and ignorance of the animal kingdom when we see how they spurn one of their number who is deformed, injured, or of a different physical appearance. It is not uncommon to see a crippled ibis shunned by the flock or a deformed kitten neglected by its mother. We stoop to this brutish, illiterate behavior when we exclude those who are different from us, or when we base our judgments on nothing more than physical characteristics.

In seventeenth-century Europe females who practiced healing arts with herbs and spices began to represent a threat to the male medical profession, which had risen in prominence under the patronage of the church. These women were accused of witchcraft. The threat spread so that any man who held a grudge against a woman could bring such an accusation against her. Women became so oppressed that they were vulnerable simply by virtue of their gender.

Bigotry is an obvious lapse of intelligent discernment. An African American by virtue of skin color, a woman by virtue of her weight or man by virtue of his height, a Jew by virtue of his ethnicity, a Muslim by virtue of her religion, all are vulnerable to the irrational judgment of those who are unable to make intelligent distinctions or judgments about intrinsic human worth.

Some religious leaders fuel the flame of religious bigotry. In the book *Christian's Response to Islam,* the author makes the self-serving claim that Christians should not try to avoid offending Muslims by leaving Jesus' name out of prayer in an ecumenical setting. If some are offended "so be it!"[2] This kind of message brings into question the purpose of prayer. Is it a public testimonial of faith or is it humble communion with the creator? Should prayer be employed as a vehicle for witness to the non-Christian? Why did Jesus go away by himself to pray? When crowds of people came to hear him, he "often withdrew to lonely places and prayed" (Luke 5:16). And Jesus' instruction to his followers was, "When you pray, go into your room, close the door and pray to your Father who is unseen" (Matthew 6:6). We have a difficult time deciding which is more important: insisting on proclaiming our own creed, or attempting to seek common ground through respectful discussion, compromise, and toleration of differences.

History records many periods of religious bigotry, which reveals how irrational human behavior can be, often based not on reality, but on imagined or false information. A measurable value of any church or political creed could be how well it imparts the principles of tolerance, compassion, and the value of all human life. These are principles that support spiritual growth, as well as mental and physical well-being. Religious observance can be a positive, life-affirming practice. Prayer, like meditation, produces resilient emotional strength. The value of corporate worship in any church can be evaluated by its ability to break barriers, to build bridges, to bring structure and moral purpose to its constituents.

The radical, ethical instruction of the Jewish carpenter is so impractical, so alien to the human spirit, that it is rarely discussed.

*If you love those who love you, what credit is that to you? Even sinners love those who love them. And if you do good to those who do good to you, even sinners do that. And if you lend to those from whom you expect repayment, what credit is that to you? Even sinners lend to sinners, expecting to be repaid in full. But love your enemies, do good to them, and lend them without expecting to get anything back. Then your reward will be great, and you will be children of the most high...Be merciful, just as your Father is merciful* (Luke 6:32-36).

This is not a teaching that is promoted in Sunday school. It is not what we teach our sons and daughters. "Stand up for your rights," we say. "Don't let anyone take advantage of you." How can anyone survive with this kind of radical religious ethic?

Believing in gun rights, legal abortion, strong borders, non-violent protest, immigration control — these are all issues we understand and can take sides on. Believing in doing good to those who mistreat you, lending without expectation of repayment, that's ridiculous. Stand up and declare that kind of morality and you'll soon be talking to yourself.

The Jewish carpenter realized this would happen. He warned his band of twelve to be careful when they entered the villages with this lesson of benevolence and forgiveness. 'It will be dangerous. You will be entering unarmed into communities that love to hate. The only way to break through that blockade is to reveal a different approach: try to demonstrate that underneath those artificial barriers is a common humanity. Your mission, if you accept it, is to show that hate does not have to beget hate. Your mission, if you can achieve it, is to create a bridge between the political alliances that give rise to division.

'But I'm warning you: what I'm asking you to do is impractical. It will put you in danger. I'm sending you like tender lambs into a slaughter house prepared to serve you up as mutton. "Therefore be as shrewd as snakes and as innocent as doves" (Matthew 10:16). Proceed with caution. Hug the surface of the earth with serpentine sinuosity, recognizing that your message is hostile to human nature.

## Notes

1 — Griffin, John Howard, *Black Like Me,* (New York, New American Library: Division of Penguin-Putnam Inc. 1962.

2 — Garlow, James L., *A Christian's Response to Islam.* (Colorado Springs, Cook Communications Ministries, 2005).

# Chapter 7

# Faith And Doubt

*Endless is the search for truth* (Laurence Sterne, 1713-1768).

*Faith keeps many doubts in her pay. If I could not doubt, I should not believe* (Henry David Thoreau).

As the former acquisition editor at CSS Publishing Company in Ohio, I gained the startling realization that an exhibitionist proclivity may induce some individuals to exhibit the most intimate details of their lives. One manuscript proposal received in my office described the life-changing experience of a man who had received a surgical implant which provided him with an erection on demand. He promised that the manuscript would be accompanied by 'before' and 'after' photos. I informed him that this would not be an appropriate subject for release from a religious publishing company.

Another offer came from a prison inmate at The Center for Forensic Psychiatry in Ann Arbor, Michigan. The proposal letter included the modest title: *Proof that God, Heaven, Jesus Christ, The Holy Ghost, Demons, and Satan all exist!*

Handwritten on a yellow legal pad, the author promised that his manuscript would provide unequivocal evidence of the existence of God.

*There are more than 1 and ½ billion Christians worldwide; and the NUMBER ONE QUESTION in the Christian Community is 'does-God-exists?' (sic) This manuscript is for OUTRIGHT—SALE for two-million-dollars or you can have it for a five-hundred-thousand-dollars advance, and a contract.*

The subject matter was more in keeping with our publishing niche than the story of the life-changing benefit of a penis implant. But I had to reject the proposal as being almost as preposterous. However, the letter was worth keeping on file these past three decades. I considered responding with a friendly explanation, providing my own thought about the "number one question in the Christian community." However, I have encountered enough zealots to observe that people who are driven to proclaim their religious convictions are rarely interested in listening to anyone else's.

History shows that when you run the risk of offending people's religious views, they are likely to respond with righteous indignation. Some of them should be confined to a psychiatric forensic center.

It was an unwelcome revelation to learn in college religion class that Moses did not really stand on Mount Sinai (or was it Mount Horeb — depending on whether you read it in Exodus or Deuteronomy) and receive the Ten Commandments from the Almighty. After all, it had been documented in that colored picture on one of the front pages of my Bible. But an understanding professor provided a soft landing by explaining that this story about Moses had an important purpose. It created a memorable narrative to pass on by word of mouth from generation to generation before the invention of the printing press. And it had some similarity to a dryly written deciphered message three centuries earlier called the Code of Hammurabi, a Babylonian code of law from Mesopotamia.

As a child in Bible school I was fascinated with the Old Testament stories. I tried to imagine the size of a boat that could hold two of every living animal, as well as enough food for all of them. And how long would that mouse survive in the hold of the ship when the anaconda came sliding along. I admit even then I was starting to be a skeptic. It was almost a relief to learn that this ancient Asian myth was being told to children long before the biblical Noah existed.

Then in a graduate school course on New Testament criticism, I learned that the four Gospels — Matthew, Mark, Luke, and John — were not written by those Apostles. In fact they were put into writing by scribal assistants after those Apostles had died. Some of those writers may never have met the Apostles under whose name they wrote. This was followed by another revelation: Paul never met Jesus face to face.

I decided to seek a different opinion from a professor at a conservative, evangelical theology school. "Well," he said, "We don't pay a lot of attention to literary criticism.[1] Our focus is on the meaning and purpose of the divinely inspired message."

"But isn't it important to let the truth about sources be known to the members of our congregations," I asked him?

"Why should we shake the foundations of people's faith? Bible scholars call these stories myths, and that confuses people."

"But we learned that the true meaning of myth is a narrative that conveys a profound truth. Shouldn't faith be grounded in truth, rather than a misunderstood history?"

And so it went. Each person has to answer that question for him or herself. For me finding out about this history of biblical literature made me want to learn more, to discover the background and meaning behind the provocative pictures in the Bible and how they had evolved from their cultural setting, to explore the mystery of human existence.

✠ ✠ ✠

The original languages in which scripture was written were Greek and Hebrew. After studying Hebrew for two years my professor in his thick Czechoslovakian accent said, "You have completed two years of studying the Hebrew language. You will forget it all in two weeks. Now you must memorize the first verses of Genesis, so that when curious Bible readers ask you about the language in which the Bible was written, you can speak Hebrew to them." I have yet to be asked to explain the language in which the Old Testament was written.

But still, that was the best advice he could have given. Other than recognizing the strange alphabet and some key words in Hebrew, I have forgotten most of the vocabulary and the grammatical construction, — except that you write and read it from right to left. However, after more than fifty years I can recite from memory the first verses of Genesis in Hebrew.

Studying more than three years of Greek was a little more practical. I discovered how translations and then translations of the translations could alter the original meaning.

Some of the biblical parables leave us scratching our heads, until we dig through the layers of interpretation. Why did Jesus get mad at a fig tree? Was Ruth's marriage to the God-fearing Boaz the result of her seduction, a story with sexual overtones and veiled symbolic language? Or was it a pragmatic decision to secure the future for herself and Naomi by marrying an older, more secure man? And what about Paul's turn around on the subject of circumcision? First he said it was fine. He even performed the procedure on Timothy, whose mother was a Jewish convert and whose father was Greek. But then he gets cool on the idea "Beware of dogs; beware of evil workers; beware of circumcision" (Philippians 3:2).

What's behind Jesus' psychic connection to a donkey? He tells his disciples to go find a donkey for him to ride into Jerusalem. After a little searching we discover that in the Old Testament (Zechariah) it is claimed that the Messiah would enter Jerusalem on a donkey. Writers of this narrative included the donkey in order to remain consistent with the Old Testament prophecy.

It's entertaining to learn what Jesus could do with pigs. I used to tell the biblical account to my children as a bed time story: when Jesus could no longer put up with a man who lived in a cave with demons, he ordered the demons out of the man. The demons begged not to be turned out, but to be sent into a herd of pigs. Jesus decided to give them what they wanted. Then the pigs ran into the water and drowned. It creates a spooky, Walt Disneyish narrative. My children loved it.

And what about some of the instructions regarding proper reverence and worship? Should we only pray in private? Are we guilty of hypocrisy if we pray in public? "But when you pray, go into your room, close the door and pray to your Father" (Matthew 6:6). Should women always cover their heads in church or refrain from speaking in church, unlike men, who are authorized to do so (I Timothy 2:9-15)? Many of these narratives reflect the cultural norms of the time in which they were written.

Because the Bible was written by many authors and has gone through many translations, its meaning is not always clear. If it is to be used for an accurate understanding of ethical philosophy or spiritual guidance, it should not be read in part, isolating a single verse or section in order to prove a point. This "proof-texting" approach has led to misunderstandings and misinterpretations. Learning about the cultural setting in which scripture was written, offers greater value and adds to our appreciation.

Before biblical scholarship became more widely accepted, many people believed that the creation story in Genesis could be read as a historical record of the earth's origin. Some biblical instructors taught that the opening chapters of the Bible were not just a spiritual and moral guide, but were a literal, historical record of how the earth was created. As biblical history became more widely understood it was evident that all the leading religions (both Christian and non-Christian) embedded their spiritual truths within legends of creation, floods, virgin births, resurrections, and second comings. These sagas were not original to our biblical writings, but were inherited from early Occidental religions, pre-dating the Judeo-Christian writings.

A 1987 ruling by the Supreme Court stated that it was not permissible for schools to teach that the world was created according to the biblical Genesis narrative. A group of conservative Christian scholars challenged this ruling by citing that microbiology is too complex to attribute organic development to natural causes or evolution alone. They explained that the complex design of such organs as the heart, the eye, and the human brain points to an "intelligent designer." They did not contest the teaching of evolution, but sought to include in public school curricula the conflict between evolution and intelligent design. To be denied this teaching, they said, would be a breach of academic freedom. George W. Bush endorsed the approach that both evolution and intelligent design should be taught.

Skepticism opens the door for compromise. It enables an individual to question his own assumptions and consider evidence that is contrary to his beliefs. Instead of remaining obdurate with intransigent conviction, skepticism is an invitation to intellectual growth; to perceive truth through accurate historical research.

Contemporary religious scholarship has provided studies that can be read by a wider secular audience. It reveals the similarities between Christianity and Islam — or the Bible and the Quran. To some uninformed Christians a claim of any commonality between the Judeo-Christian teachings and the Islamic writings could be disturbing, maybe even considered heresy.

A friend, who was searching for spiritual enlightenment, told me that he had asked his pastor if it would be helpful to read the Quran, in order to become more informed about the nature of Islam. The minister warned him not to read this dangerous literature. It might mislead him. It was as though the pastor was speaking to an impressionable third grader who might be lured into an Islamic conversion. If my friend had decided to defy that minister, he would have discovered that much of what we are told about Islamic scriptures is false propaganda. There is no duty to kill infidels and in fact there is no reference to Sharia law.

Dr. Garry Wills, a Pulitzer Prize winning author of forty books, has studied the Quran and has produced an incisive book about its teachings: *What the Qur'an Meant and why it Matters*. He advises that any serious study of religion must include a reading of the Quran.

How can one expect the gospel, the radical message of the New Testament, to be instructive if it is reduced to pablum that serves only to comfort and to confirm unchallenged prejudice? When we confront it honestly, it has the power to transform, to remove the scales from our solipsistic eyes. From it we gain the wisdom to understand and accept the diversity of approaches that lead to enlightenment.

The content of our Bible as we know it was determined by human debate and consensus. To this day there is no common agreement as to what is officially considered Old Testament scripture. The question of what should be in the Bible has been referred to as a lingering illness.

There were dozens of gospels and epistles in circulation during the first couple centuries A.D. Gradually a procedure emerged to determine which should be considered authentic (canonical) and which should be rejected. One of the earliest tests to authenticate New Testament content was whether the writings were actually the *ipsissima verba* of Jesus. These "sayings of Jesus" had circulated orally and were also written down in collections of sayings, notably in one of the Gnostic writings, the Gospel of Thomas. Subsequently the letters of Paul were added, but only if they had developed a history of being read in worship services. To some scholars this seems like a slipshod procedure for determining authenticity: in other words, the more widely a message is read and heard, the more legitimate it becomes.

Finally, around the year 200 A.D. the church fathers made the decision to eliminate all but four of the many gospels that were in circulation at the time, namely only those gospels attributed to Matthew, Mark, Luke, and John.

Debate about the content of both old and new testaments continued through the centuries. In 1546, the Council of Trent, in response to the Protestant Reformation, included such books as Tobit, Judith, Maccabees, Ecclesiasticus, and Wisdom of Solomon. Many members of Protestant churches may never have heard of these titles.

Thirteen years later (1559), the Reformed churches decided that these books should not be included in the Protestant Bible. In 1580 Lutherans allowed these titles to be included, but only as an appendix. In 1950 the Orthodox Church chose some of them and eliminated others.

In light of this squabbling, it seems prudent to maintain a skeptical judgment toward any claim of infallibility of scriptural writings. Surely these were sincere, dedicated believers who determined the content of our Bible. But we should remain cautious of accepting indiscriminately any claims that these writings must be considered divinely inspired or the infallible word of God.

✛ ✛ ✛

If we should happen to read in the Quran a story like the following, we would be justifiably leery about the violent threat of the Islamic culture:

*When the trumpets sounded, the army shouted, and at the sound of the trumpet, when the men gave a loud shout, the wall collapsed; so everyone charged straight in, and they took the city. They devoted the city to the Lord and destroyed with the sword every living thing in it—men and women, young and old, cattle, sheep and donkeys.*

Some individuals reading the Christian Bible for the first time might become shaken by its language and violence. There are disturbing passages that deserve cautious interpretation. These verses above from the Old Testament (Joshua 6:20-21) would alarm us if we read them in the Quran. What kind of religion boasts of mass killing, including children and innocent livestock?

Those who grew up in non-Christian cultures have asked, "Is this Christian God a vengeful tyrant? This does not sound like a benevolent, loving creator." Their criticism is prompted by those biblical writings that call for genocide or total annihilation. In First Samuel God commands the utter destruction of the Amalekites, 'all that they have...do not spare them, but kill both man and woman, infant and nursing child, ox and sheep, camel and donkey.' When Saul failed to follow through on that command, God took away his kingdom.

We humans can be savage beasts. Nothing in nature is so well equipped for hurting or hating as a human being. "I praise you because I am fearfully and wonderfully made" (Psalm 139:14). We are capable of retaliation and savagery. Confuse or frighten us and we are capable of thrashing you. Put us into crowded tenements and we will rob each other. Take something away from us and we will retaliate. Impoverish us and we will burn down our own cities in the night. Excite us, frighten us, anger us and we can become more destructive than swarms of locusts or a streak of tigers.

Human passion can lead to destruction. Beliefs become dangerous when they are intolerant of doubt. Faith that leaves no room for skepticism can go down a dangerous path of certitude. Any religion that promotes violence must be held in suspicion.

Biblical literature has not always given the wisest instruction when it comes to the treatment of women. In the first book of the Bible, two angels disguised as strangers are guests in Lot's house. Some men in the town come to the house. They want Lot to send out the strangers so that they can use them as they would use a woman. Lot attempts to protect his guests by making a grotesque offer: "I have two daughters who have not known a man; let me bring them out to you, and you may do to them as you wish" (Genesis 19: 1-8). This is one of the more disturbing biblical passages, a despicable example of an evil father. It reminds us that these narratives emerged from a culture not far removed from primitive savagery. Their survival called for brutality and violence and their god was one who took sides with them and advised them to dispose of alien tribes.

Deuteronomy 22:20-21 delivers a stern message about the significance of a woman's virginity. If a man marries her and discovers that she is not a virgin, then she should be brought out and stoned to death by the men of her city.

In other words, if she has engaged in premarital sex, she should be killed.

The Old Testament book of Judges describes the brutal sacrifice of a woman who is raped and then cut into twelve pieces, limb by limb." (This violent narrative is similar to the one described in Genesis 19). None of these stories will we hear in a worship setting. But awareness of them helps us become more objective and less self-righteous about the purity of our Judeo-Christian heritage.

Slavery was condoned in ancient cultures and some Bible verses reflect this acceptance. "And if a man beats his male or female servant with a rod, so that he dies, he shall be punished. Notwithstanding, if he remains alive a day or two, he shall not be punished for he (the slave) is his property." This was a favorite verse of slave owners. All of Exodus 21 talks about rules for treating slaves.

The New Testament admonishes "Servants, be submissive to your master with all fear, not only to the good and gentle, but also to the harsh" (1 Peter 2:18).

Does the Old Testament give an account of an omnipotent creator, or is it a series of tales that are created to explain (possibly even justify) human destruction and hatred? Before we pass judgment on Islam, we should be aware that our Judeo-Christian literature is more violent than the whole of the Quran. Yet if we saw these same verses in the Quran, we would be horrified and claim that Islam was an evil religion and that Muslims should not be trusted: fodder for Christian bigotry. Better understanding of our own biblical literature makes us more tolerant and understanding of other faiths and the scriptures which have evolved from their cultural backgrounds.

When we put into practice the tenets of our religion, we are tempted to do so with unspoken assumptions of exclusivity. What is the subtle implication of our nationalistic plea, "God Bless America?" Are we beseeching divine blessing on our country exclusive of others? Does it suggest a xenophobic prejudice that God must look more favorably on

Americans than on Koreans, or Chinese, or Kenyans? What about the peasants of Iran, the Hindus of India, the natives of Africa, the inhabitants of Europe? Do we assume, like the ancient Hebrews, that God looks with more favor upon our nation than others? Could we implore God to "bless all mankind?" Is it unpatriotic to ask whether we are preaching nationalistic allegiance above humanitarian justice and ethical pragmatism?

We elevate national symbols to reverential devotion. Yet we are willfully blind to the consequences of where nationalist fervor can take us. We attack with fascist furor any who employ the democratically protected right to peaceful protest. We are more loyal to the symbols of our national identity than to those of our religious heritage. We condemn anyone who will not stand at attention to honor the United States flag or sing the national anthem, reminiscent of the condemnation imposed on those who protested the swastika in Nazi Germany. We display ignorance about our own constitutional history: that over seventy years ago the Supreme Court ruled that children in public schools cannot and should not be forced to salute the flag or pledge allegiance to it. "Words uttered under coercion are proof of loyalty to nothing but self-interest," wrote Justices Hugo Black and William O. Douglas. These are hard-earned democratic freedoms for which blood has been shed.

Madeleine Albright, former secretary of state and US Ambassador to the United Nations, has pointed out Donald Trump's puzzling attraction to fascist rulers. Rodrigo Duterte, head of the Philippine government, has encouraged enforcement officers to kill over ten thousand of the most disadvantaged people in his country. Trump telephoned Duterte to congratulate him for doing an "unbelievable job."[2]

He claims that Egyptian general Abdel Fattah el-Sisi is "fantastic," even though the Egyptian government is shutting down public debate, using deadly force against protesters, criticizing news media and outlawing political opposition.

He congratulated Turkish President Erdogan in the same year that Erdogan changed the Turkish constitution enabling him to remain in office without opposition over the next ten years.

Surprisingly, he also commends autocrats who commit murder in order to retain their control. About North Korea's Kim Jong-un he said, "You have to give him credit. How many young guys — he was like 26 or 25 when his father died — take over these tough generals, and all of a sudden... he's the boss. It's incredible. He wiped out the uncle. He wiped out this one, that one. I mean, this guy doesn't play games." He praised Vladimir Putin as "a man so highly respected within his own country and beyond." Meanwhile, he has condemned most of our country's institutions: the US courts, the FBI, the US press and media, and our election system. This is unprecedented language from a president of our country.

President Trump's impulsive approach to governing can be disturbing, although he has implemented a number of changes by executive order that appeal to his base of supporters. The deregulation of car-emissions standards will reduce consumer costs by over $500 billion. The Transportation Agency estimates that the Trump mileage changes could increase global temperatures by 0.003 percent by the year 2100, or essentially by zero. Many landowners celebrate the Interior Department proposed changes to the Endangered Species Act. The new ruling by the Health and Human Services Department allows more insurance options for millions of Americans. The Senate authorized a $717 billion defense bill which provides troops the largest pay increase in nine years. The unreflective masses consider the validation of political success to be the measure of economic gains. The tax reduction act brought substantial stock market gains in early 2018. However, those gains may eventually evaporate as the threat of tariffs and their global consequences take effect over the next few years.

The president's Twitter messages detract from the positive news he might be able to elicit from these right wing achievements. Even his strongest editorial defenders claim that his Twitter rampages hinder his ability to project a positive message.

The general public is willing to overlook moral turpitude if it benefits their pocket books, although at the time of this writing the verdict is still out as to how much damage the trade wars might inflict on the American economy and the prices Americans pay for non-discretionary goods. Economists from the London School of Economics proved as far back as 1936 that tariffs on imports penalize the country that imposes them. That was illustrated in the early 1930s when the Smoot-Hawley Tariff Act contributed to the worst economic depression in American history. Tariffs reduce overall growth and reshape the economy. Several U.S. companies are planning to shift their production to Canada and Europe to avoid higher reciprocal tariffs. Harley Davidson plans to move some of its production to Europe eliminating hundreds of U.S. jobs; BMW says that foreign retaliation will reduce the export of their cars from its South Carolina plant. The Texas Alliance of Energy Producers says that higher costs of steel due to the tariffs will hurt drilling and production of oil, the biggest U.S. export success story of recent years.

A manufacturer served by a company where I am the board chairman was praised in 2017 by President Trump for its dedication to maintaining American jobs. A few months after that recognition by the president, the manufacturer informed our company that they were transferring to China all the assembly work we were performing for them at our division in the United States. Our company had to lay off over twenty percent of our Illinois employees, and compensation of officers was reduced.

Most people of both political parties feel that Republican Senator John McCain and other Vietnam veterans were justified in rejecting Donald Trump's boasting of bravery for surviving the risks of sexually transmitted diseases. "It's like Vietnam. It is my personal Vietnam. I feel like a great and very brave solder," he told Howard Stern. Stern agreed that "every vagina is like a potential land mine."[3] Never before has a president made light of military bravery with this type of language. Conservative, evangelical Christian groups have turned a blind eye to his crude language, his claims of sexual prowess, and his misogynistic approach to women because of his positions on immigration and abortion, which hold higher sway than moral behavior for some Republican voters.

The president's core supporters treat him with reverential bias. He has been called the savior of conservative causes by his most sympathetic followers. When I have attempted to question one of the president's judgments, my skepticism has been met with malevolent rancor by those who support him. Their sudden hostility at the mention of any word of criticism exposes the challenge in defending the president's duplicity and intellectual shallowness. Many of his defenders see him as "the common man who talks like me." Trump has stated more than once, "I love the poorly educated." When his ignorance of American constitutional history is pointed out, he distracts attention from it by pointing a finger at Barack Obama. (As a pundit said, "Pity George Washington; he couldn't blame it on the previous administration.")

When political philosophy is characterized by intolerance of opposing opinions, democracy is diminished and civil rights are weakened. To proclaim that peaceful protestors should be kicked out of our country is an indication either of ignorance of American history, or an egregious display of fascism. Republican leaders have urged the president to use caution before demanding that a football team owner should "get that son of a bitch off the field now" when a player knelt for the national anthem, an act which has nothing to do with military allegiance. His motive was called into question when it was revealed that he had confided to the owner of the NFL team that his real reason for taking this stand was driven by the political popularity he thought it brought him. He exclaimed to Dallas Cowboys owner Jerry Jones that "You can't win this one. This is a very big winning issue for me...This one lifts *me!*"

Ironically, protest is muted — if not silent — when a photograph of a crucifix in a glass of urine appears in a national museum. When Andres Serrano submitted his photograph of the plastic crucifix in a glass tank of his own urine, it was chosen as the winner of the Southeastern Center for Contemporary Arts "Awards in the Visual Arts" category. This program is sponsored by the National Endowment for the Arts, a United States government agency that offers tax supported funding for artistic projects. Your taxes and mine paid for this questionable piece of "art." The Houston Museum of Contemporary Arts held a four month display of the image alongside a jumbo portrait of the President. No one complained. No one protested. Our tribal identity with the symbols of America abandons rational consideration and subverts the value of biblical — or even culturally acceptable — ethics.

Sectarian loyalty is antithetical to the core teaching of New Testament ethics. The most audacious ethical teaching of the New Testament is one that is not often mentioned: the instruction to carry out radical love, which knows no national or racial barriers.

*You have heard that it was said, 'Love your neighbor and hate your enemy.' But I tell you: Love your enemies and pray for those who persecute you, that you may be sons of your Father in heaven'...If you love those who love you, what reward will you get? Are not even the tax collectors doing that? And if you greet only your brothers, what are you doing more than others? Do not even pagans do that?* (Matthew 5:43-48).

This radical ethic is not conducive to survival in our world of homicidal humanity. It probably would not befit the ruler of a country. But its message encourages personal restraint. You were wronged? You want to hit back? You want to destroy? Slow down, this gospel implores. Look for another option. An eye for an eye is out of date. A tooth for a tooth? Soon we would all be blind and toothless. New Testament ethical teaching assumes that we are capable of rising above our desperate urge for retaliation. Anyone can return hate for hate. There is no glory in that kind of behavior. Anyone can strike back. There is no honor in that. But introduce compassion into the battle of conflict and you will become recognized as one who lives by a sanctified moral philosophy.

On October 2, 2006, Charles Roberts entered an Amish schoolhouse in Nickle Mines, Pennsylvania, with a hand gun, a 12-gauge shotgun, a rifle, and two knives. He ordered the teacher and the boys to leave the room. He then bound the legs of ten young school girls and had them stand up against the blackboard. In revenge for a slight he had suffered twenty years earlier, he shot all the girls, then pointed the handgun at his head and killed himself. Six of the girls, aged 6 to 13, died and the others were seriously wounded.

The stunning part of this story was the reaction of the Amish community. They walked as a group to the home of Charles Roberts' widow to offer their prayers and forgiveness. They attended the funeral of the murderer and in the days following showered his wife with gifts, meals, and love (Matthew 5:43-48). Their actions speak more loudly than the boldest church sermon.

Roberts' mother and father thought that they would have to move far away. What community would ever accept them for raising such an evil son? But later in the day an Amish man came to their home with a message: we know you are grieving the loss of your child just as we are.

On the day of the funeral thirty Amish men and women, some the parents of the girls who had been murdered, attended to offer their support and condolences.

Years later the Amish continue to struggle every day with the need to forgive. In one home a sixteen year old girl sits in a wheelchair, unable to move, to speak or feed herself. A twenty-three year old man sits in the same room at a table. He is unable to speak, not because he can't, but because he still struggles with the emotional shock and pain he has felt every day since.

✚ ✚ ✚

We were taught in Bible school to sing, "Red and yellow, black and white, they are equal in his sight." We stopped singing that after age seven. The message never carried over into our adult teaching.

David Crosby, the singer-songwriter of Crosby, Stills & Nash, has written about the time when he first heard the song "Strange Fruit" sung by the Negro blues artist Josh White. Crosby didn't understand the meaning of the words, so he asked his mother, who loved folk music, to explain the meaning of the words. She sat down with tears in her eyes and said, "I don't want to have to tell you this." Crosby says he got scared. She told him, "Davey, some people don't like other people because of their skin." Crosby said, "That doesn't make any sense." And she told him, "Yes, you're right, but they don't. It's called racial prejudice and it's wrong." She went on to explain that the meaning of "strange fruit" was about black people being hung from trees by white people.[4]

✚ ✚ ✚

I stood in front of a bakery counter deciding on a choice of pastry to eat with my coffee. After I made my selection, I changed my mind and told the dour-faced clerk that I wanted a different pastry. She glared at me with contempt, and made the exchange with exaggerated irritation. I was not in the mood to accept her disdain for such a simple request.

"I am so sorry to disturb you," I said sarcastically. "For some reason I made the wild assumption that you worked here to serve the customer.

It was not a nice thing to say. My wife was embarrassed. But my anger flared at her insolence. How would I survive in a world where this happened every day? How would I tolerate injustice if I lived in a different skin…or wore a turban?

This year a white employee of a Starbucks in Pennsylvania called the police to report two young black men who used the restroom before they had placed their order.

(How many times have I walked into a restaurant to use the restroom without ordering?) An employee at a New Jersey gym called the police and reported that two black men had not paid to use the facility. If he had checked further he would have found that they had paid. A woman in California called the police on three black women about whom she was suspicious. They were carrying bags out of a house they had rented on Airbnb. A white Yale student called the police on a black graduate student who was resting in a common area. She thought he looked "suspicious."

When I consider how sensitive I have been to unkind or even impatient treatment, I fear that I would not survive in this country as a minority or a person of color. My response to biased treatment would result in a black eye or a trip to jail.

I accompanied a friend to a modest, back-alley body shop where I had previously taken my car for repair. My friend needed a minor alteration performed on his car. The owner came out to look at the car. He said, "who is this for?" I said, "For him," pointing to my friend. The owner said, "I don't do that kind of work." He turned around and went back inside his building.

We went to another location where they sell used interior car seats and accessories like the ones my friend was looking for. I told the manager, we need a back seat for the van. "Whose van," he asked? I pointed to my friend. He said, "We don't have anything like that." (We could see through the side office door a warehouse filled floor to ceiling with used car and van seats.) Maybe we should have protested. But when you're not sure you take the easiest escape route. We walked out. Neither of us made a comment, but it was an awkward moment.

I began to realize that my friend possessed more power than I. The power of self-control. I lacked the civility to tolerate the disdain of the woman at the pastry counter. My friend, on the other hand, has a nobility of spirit, the result of generations of sufferance. He is a musician who has shared the stage with David Sanborn, Slide Hampton, performed with Duke Ellington, Woody Herman, and the Ray

Charles bands. He has been cheered in Italy, honored in Singapore and Japan, celebrated in Egypt. In his own country he is often snubbed. I try to understand the mind of someone who judges a person by color, and is blind to character. Some dismiss it as white privilege. Maybe that's the wrong term. Maybe there's a different, more patient, non-violent way to bring attention to this injustice — like kneeling for the anthem. Of course that may be offensive to some white folks. But then, some actions are more offensive than others. Because...

"There was a time when I believed in an arc of cosmic justice, that good acts were rewarded and bad deeds punished...I would like to believe in God. I simply can't. The reasons are physical. When I was nine, some kid beat me up for amusement, and when I came home crying to my father, his answer — *Fight that boy or fight me* — was godless, because it told me that there was no justice in the world, save the justice we dish out with our own hands. When I was twelve, six boys jumped off the number 28 bus headed to Mondawmin Mall, threw me to the ground, and stomped on my head. But what struck me most that afternoon was not those boys but the godless, heathen adults walking by. Down there on the ground, my head literally being kicked in, I understood: No one, not my father, not the cops, and certainly not anyone's God, was coming to save me. The world was brutal -..."[5]

As I read page after page of this African American author's personal experience and how it related to the eight years of Barack Obama's presidency, I began to feel viscerally assaulted. I had to read it in small doses. I realized how unknowingly privileged I was. How convenient: I could put the book down and walk away. Some encounter it every time they open their door and go out to brave the world.

✠ ✠ ✠

I wonder. Does it ever occur to those good folks to question their own judgments? Are they capable of skepticism, or do they only see these issues as being either *my* way or the wrong way? Is it about drawing attention to themselves and their superiority?

David Trinko, an editor with the Lima (Ohio) News has written that "After doing this job for a dozen years, I've noticed something disconcerting. People just aren't as civil as they once were." (*Lima News*, Sunday, June 24, 2018). Political discourse is conducted with name-calling and offensive slurs. It emanates from the highest office in Washington, D.C.

How could theological instruction respond to this attitude? Could we highlight those teachings that inspire humility? Could we create an ecclesiastical fellowship in which intolerance, self-righteous judgment, and bigotry are unacceptable? Such a gathering would stand alone as a beacon of hope within our increasingly divided culture.

✛ ✛ ✛

My skepticism regarding the literal interpretation of scripture is not an indication of arrogant denial of its relevance to faith. I have no intention of diminishing its value. On the contrary I view it critically because of how it has shaped my life. Skepticism motivates me to remove the layers of cultural accretion, to turn from the lens of naïve piety, and try to understand how those biblical ancestors sought the answers to difficult questions…how they went about seeking Truth.

How did their culture address issues that affect us today? Are their answers appropriate for us to follow? What did they have to say about values that are worth living and dying for? (Luke 12:13-21; 1 Corinthians 13).

What about the appropriation of money, taxation? (Mark 14:3-11).

What was their teaching about unfairness? (Matthew 18:21-35).

Were they tempted to hang onto possessions the way I am? (Luke 12:13-21).

What do these thousand pages say about suicide? There were those who suffered total despair, to the point of wishing they had never been born (Ecclesiastes 7:17b).

Did they consider it acceptable to have tattoos? (Leviticus 19:28).

Were they vegetarians? Our ancestors who lived between the Stone Age and the first agricultural period may have gotten most of their nutrition from gathered fruits and nuts. The opening verses of the Bible would suggest that the vegetarian diet was adequate (Genesis 1:29-30).

When this body of literature is taken seriously it deepens our understanding of the cultural influences which affected the meaning and ultimate message. Awareness of the imperfections encourages us to be less judgmental about the religious literature of other cultures. However, as we labor through the chapters of both Old and New Testaments, we are also drawn into the beauty, poetry and inspiration of the Psalms. We are confronted with the challenge to subdue sanctimonious religious pride and practice humility, sacrifice, and benevolence.

These admonitions may be humanly unattainable. But while they may be impossible to achieve, we become aware of the capacity, the possibility, of being transformed when we admit our weakness and accept them as a gift.

## Notes

1 — Literary criticism, or biblical criticism, does not refer to disapproval or fault-finding. Biblical criticism is conducted by those devoted to understanding the writings of the Bible as they relate to its cultural setting, grammar, and style.

2 — Albright, Madeleine, *Fascism: A Warning*, (NewYork, HarperCollins Publishers, 2018).

3 — Singer, Mark, *Trump and Me*, *(NewYork*, Penguin Random House, 2016).

4 — Crosby, David. Editorial "A Song of Horror," in Wall Street Journal, Saturday / Sunday, February 24-25, 2018.

5 — Coates, Ta-Nehisi, *We Were Eight Years in Power: An American Tragedy*, (New York, One World, 2017).

# Chapter 8

# You Are Dying, But Not Right Now...

*Let me not pray to be sheltered from dangers but to be
fearless in facing them.
Let me not beg for the stilling of my pain but for the
heart to conquer it.
Let me not look for allies in life's battlefield but to my
own strength.
Let me not crave in anxious fear to be saved but hope
for the patience to win my freedom.
Grant me that I may not be a coward, feeling your
mercy in my success alone; but let me find the grasp
of your hand in my failure.*
Rabindranath Tagore, *Fruit Gathering*

Tombstones provide a final opportunity to get even, vent frustration, or give a chuckle to a casual observer. Wandering through a cemetery in Connecticut, I came across the grave marker of a perturbed fellow who wanted his family to remember his warning, *I told you I was sick!*

In the village of Rimer, Ohio the tombstone of a hard working quarryman is inscribed with the words by which he wished to be remembered: *I've dredged and sledged stone all my life, but I'll never dredge and sledge the stone above me now.* That was the calm admission that he had no false hopes of a reincarnation.

A Purple Heart-decorated member of the Air Force became the first gay member of the U.S. military to publicly out himself. Following his revelation, he was unsuccessful in his attempt to keep his military job and his case was featured on the front cover of *Time* magazine in 1975. He was buried at the Congressional Cemetery in Washington, DC. The inscription on his grave stone is: *When I was in the military they gave me a medal for killing two men, and a discharge for loving one.*

Some stones are inscribed with curses nursed to the final breath. Others take advantage of a last chance to get even. Cecil Eads died in 1993. He wanted no one to forget what he thought of his sibling by having this inscription carved on his stone: *My brother was good at pissing people off.*

One grave stone hinted at the unfortunate ending of a married man: *Ma loves pa — Pa loves women. Ma caught pa, with two in swimming — Here lies pa.*

A woman named Kay had her complete fudge recipe inscribed on her tombstone, under which was written *Wherever she goes, there's laughter.*

Edith Barlow, who died in 1991, wanted her friends to know that she was strong enough to deal with whatever fate handed her. After all, *Shit happens* she had inscribed on her tomb stone.

Russell Larsen's gravestone epitaph is one that is apparently well-known to cowboys: *Two things I love most, good horses and beautiful women, and when I die, I hope they tan this old hide of mine and make it into a lady's riding saddle, so I can rest in peace between the two things I love the most.*

And then there are Frances and Wayne Thatcher whose tomb stone contains the macabre wording *Damn it's dark down here.*

I heard an older woman comment that, "The mirror used to be my friend, now it's my assassin." While many cultures celebrate aging and venerate their elders, our Western society idolizes youthfulness. We view aging as a problem, a deficiency that needs to be treated. Advertisers focus attention on youth and promote products that will keep us trying forever to look like teenage senior citizens. Because of our distaste for the appearance of aging, we hide our elderly away in nursing homes or retirement centers.

Other cultures might help us modify this view. The Greek word for "old man" isn't a negative description. It's a symbol of honor. Respect for elders was an accepted virtue. At my age this philosophy has a pleasant ring.

We could have learned this lesson from the Native Americans before we corralled them into reservations. The wisdom of their elderly was venerated and was sought for resolving disputes within their society.

My Lebanese friend, Gibran, told me that while nursing homes exist in his native country, they are inhabited only by those who have no family members to care for them. Their culture assumes it is the responsibility of younger family members to care for the aging.

The Confucian principle of family piety has influenced the Korean culture, where respect for parents is an accepted way of life. Young family members are expected to take care of the elderly in the family. In China reverence for one's elders is a duty. It would be considered dishonorable to put a family member in a retirement home. Likewise, in India the advice from the elderly is sought for everything from investments to wedding plans.

These cultures have nurtured the custom of viewing aging as a well-earned badge of endurance. The wrinkled skin, the bald heads are seen as signs of ripening.

Our American culture connects aging with death, and we have placed a taboo on dying, protecting our children from its appearance, hiding it in hospitals, and medically attempting to delay its inevitability.

When a young police detective's wife was dying of cancer, I was called to their house to counsel the family's two young children and talk to the dying girl. While her condition was clearly terminal, the family around her was attempting to comfort her by telling her that she was going to get better. This betrayal of trust left her highly agitated. No one seemed capable of discussing with her the reality of her imminent death. She knew they were not being forthcoming; her only comfort was the morphine pump at her finger tip. (Research indicates that when patients control their own pain medication they don't use as much of it; and yet report less suffering.)

As I sat by her side I noticed how restless and nervous she was. I held her hand, stroked her arm gently. I said to her, "You and I both know that you are going to die. But it's not happening right now. You can relax now." She opened her eyes and looked at me intently. She saw that I was telling her the truth. Her muscles slackened. Her face softened. Hearing a voice that shared her reality absorbed the loneliness. She did not need diversion and denial. She needed to hear the truth. I sat by her bedside for many hours. She died peacefully the next day.

There is a cultural uneasiness surrounding death. We often surround the dying person with unrealistic hope, losing the opportunity in those critical moments for shared awareness of one of life's most natural events. There is no need for mystical pronouncements. Sitting peacefully with people who are dying can lead toward an enlightened connection.

Sherwin Nuland, in his book *How We Die*[1], says that doctors are reluctant to talk frankly with patients about death. They confess that they hesitate to reveal the imminent death of their patient, lest they take away hope. But in so doing, they deprive the dying patient of any final closure with loved ones.

I stood by the hospital bedside with the elderly parents of a forty-five year old daughter who was dying of brain cancer. A Pentecostal minister was on the other side of the bed praying in a booming voice, which attracted the attention of nurses in the hallway: "O God, we put all our faith in you. We trust you, Lord. God, we just come here as your humble servants. God, we pray for a MIR-A-CUL. We just know that you can heal this girl, your faithful servant. We just ask you to raise her, God, like you did LAZ-A-RUS. God, just bring us a MIR-A-CUL. God…"

This style of prayer employs the frequent use of the word "just" as in "what is morally our right anyway." And the repetitious use of the Lord's name makes it abundantly clear who is being addressed; namely the almighty, not those who are standing around the bedside, although the booming voice and dramatic gestures might expose some duplicity of intention.

I stayed with the parents a long time after the girl fell asleep. She never woke up. The preacher was surely sincere in his devout efforts to call on God for healing, but was he setting the parent's up for a challenge to their faith? Isn't God supposed to answer prayers? Why did He let them down? If, through divine intervention, you could heal the sick in the first century, why not in the twentieth?

Coming to terms with death is a great teaching moment. All our striving is vanity. Our worry about status and reputation — all of it is deceit, judgment, and criticism. A minister's job is not to prove that heaven exists, but to help people survive life's complexities, and face uncertain futures.

A woman comes to me and says: "My helpless, innocent child died in a fire at the babysitter's house while I was at work. I can't believe in a God who would let that happen."

I could respond by attempting to prove to her that God had nothing to do with it and talk to her about God's nature, the sacrifice of his own son. Or…I could put my head down and listen with tears of sympathy and grief as she shared this heart-wrenching story. The first might satisfy my own need to feel worthy of my profession. The second would be a response to her need, evidence of a compassionate understanding. God is capable of defending Himself.

## Religion And Mental Health

The church and her teachers have not always been tolerant of those seeking truth. In the seventeenth century the church taught with absolute conviction that the sun moved around the earth, and that this was verified by holy scriptures. Therefore, to challenge this pronouncement was a sin against biblical faith and the teaching of the church.

Galileo knew that this was a false conception of the cosmos. He taught the Copernican model of the universe, in which the sun was at the center. For this, Galileo was condemned by the church Office of Heresy in 1633. "We pronounce, judge, and declare, that you, the said Galileo…

have rendered yourself vehemently suspected by the Holy Office of Heresy, that is, of having believed and held the doctrine (which is false and contrary to the holy and divine scriptures) that the sun is the center of the world, and that it does not move from east to west, and that the earth does not move, and is not the center of the world. We condemn thee to the prison of the holy office…and so as salutary penance we enjoin on thee that for the space of three years thou shalt recite once a week the Seven Penitential Psalms."[2]

Galileo agreed not to teach "heresy" and spent the rest of his life under house arrest. Giordano Bruno was not as fortunate as Galileo. He went beyond Copernicus and taught that the universe was infinite, consisting of other planets, which might even contain life. For this heresy the church authorities condemned him to be burned at the stake. This was in 1600, 33 years before Galileo was likewise condemned.

George Fox, the seventeenth-century founder of the Society of Friends, commonly known as the Quakers, traveled through England and later North America proclaiming what he believed were the pure principles of Christian faith. Because his teachings were often contradictory to the tenants of the established church, he was imprisoned for blasphemy for refusing to swear an oath of allegiance to Britain.

The case for biblical accuracy has been weakened in previous periods by clerics who insisted on a literal interpretation of the scriptures. James Woodrow, the uncle of President Woodrow Wilson, claimed that there was no contradiction between the theory of evolution and the biblical story of creation. Because of this claim he was asked to resign from his post at Columbia Theological School. He refused and two years later was tried for heresy. The case created such controversy that Columbia was forced to close their doors for the 1887-1888 school year. The Presbyterian Church remained staunch against evolution until 1969, when it simply became impossible to ignore scientific evidence.

History is replete with religious founders who were ridiculed, punished, and often imprisoned for advancing a religious doctrine that was out of the mainstream. Jehovah Witnesses, for example, have encountered opposition because of their refusal to accept life-saving blood transfusions.

Psychiatric journals include descriptions of religious phobias, or fears that create abnormal anxiety. *Islamophobia* is a disorder that needs little explanation. This dislike or hatred of Islam and Muslims is met on the other side by *Christophobics*, who fear or hate Christians, or anything that represents Christianity. *Atheophobia* afflicts anyone with an irrational hatred of atheists. We human beings identify ourselves with those who think and believe as we do. We are unsettled when we run into someone who has a different religious or political conviction. The brave, daring, and curious are willing to step outside the tribal compound and explore what's there. Those who do, find that it's a fascinating adventure.

✠ ✠ ✠

A man rises from his place in church and begins speaking incoherently. Is he speaking in tongues or is he displaying a psychotic episode?

At a tiny, backwoods church on the southern tip of West Virginia, I watch the minister take the lid off a box that is writhing with poisonous vipers. The box is on the floor in front of the altar. Men and women walk to the front, pick up the snakes, hold them above their heads and wrap them around their necks. A large, barrel-chested man takes a mason jar of strychnine from the altar, puts it to his mouth, and swallows. The ritual is done in the name of scripture, specifically Mark 16:18: "And these signs will accompany those who believe: In my name they will cast out demons; they will speak in new tongues; they will pick up serpents, and if they drink any deadly thing, it will not hurt them..." Except when it does. Several have died in this little back woods congregation from snake bites and consumptive strychnine. (See the chapter "Varieties Of Worship" for a more complete description of this type of worship.)

Faithful Protestants and Catholics have for centuries accepted a doctrine that anyone outside their own traditions might view with skepticism, if not disgust. In the year 1215 AD the Roman Catholic Church officially adopted the doctrine of transubstantiation. During a worship service the priest utters words of consecration over a chalice of wine and a plate of wafers. As the words are spoken, the elements become the flesh and blood of Christ, even though they appear to be unaltered. Although this practice refers to the Last Supper that Jesus celebrated with his disciples, there is no basis in scripture to support this radical transformation. Lutheran and most Protestant denominations teach that the true body and blood of Christ are very much present "in, with, and under" the bread and wine. (Martin Luther taught that this mysterious presence of Christ is beyond explanation.) Most of us who have grown up in the church participate in this tradition with little thought about the doctrinal struggles behind it. We accept it as a form of corporate worship, assuring us of forgiveness for our sins. But it's little wonder that those from other cultures, who hear about our sacrament of Holy Communion for the first time, apply to us the titles cannibal, blood guzzler, or carnivorous beasts. And we think snake worshipping is strange!

Where is the line between faith and delusion, or between malice and mental illness? Sigmund Freud claimed that religion was "blissful hallucinatory confusion." He compared Christian teaching to an "obsessive compulsive neurosis." Contemporary authors like Richard Dawkins and Sam Harris have continued to express the theory that religious faith is a psychological defect or sickness.

But spiritual faith has had proponents among the psychiatric profession. Harvard professor, Tyler VanderWeele, collaborated in the research and publication of several studies that identify the link between religious worship and enhanced health. Participation in corporate worship, for example, has been shown to reduce mortality by about thirty percent over a sixteen year period, and a five-fold reduction in the likelihood of suicide. Depression is much less likely among church worshippers. Regular participation in religious worship is also associated with more healthy social relationships and stable marriages. Compared to the non-church affiliated, church members revealed a higher life satisfaction, they are more generous in charitable giving, and are more involved in community service activities.

Harold Koenig, MD, a psychiatrist at the Duke University Medical Center, is the author several books which illustrate how religious involvement is connected with dramatically lower substance abuse and suicide. Spiritually disciplined people respond better to the treatment of stress-related disorders and dementia.

This, of course, does not provide proof for doctrinal claims. But it refutes those who say that religious faith is an illness, and it supports the evidence that faith contributes to physical health, longevity, and a sense of well-being.

Religion, like nuclear energy, which can produce either bombs or electricity, can be employed in the service of either good or evil. Churches that are experiencing growth today are the most inclusive. Acceptance is the dominant theme, where tolerance and love and nonjudgment are promoted.

When an ecclesiastical organization or its leaders lay claim to an inspired source of doctrine or infallibility, ratified by a supernatural power, they lay the groundwork for disruption and conflict. When admitting its human limitations, religious doctrine retains the humility necessary to seek mutual values rather than dominance. Spiritual leaders can serve a higher purpose when they build bridges and search for common humanity rather than demanding adherence to sovereign claims. The skeptic can pledge loyalty to a spiritual membership and derive the blessings and benefits of that association, without claiming superiority over those who may define their creed with a contrary doctrinal vocabulary.

When we read the newspaper accounts of a school shooter, the individual is often described as "a loner," someone who could not fit in, could not find a place of belonging. Psychologists describe this need to belong as a fundamental requirement of mental stability.

We find security and comfort in the group with which we identify. Our peers influence how we think and act, how we dress and speak. Compare the members of a motorcycle club — their tattoos, conversation, and leather jackets — with the dress and behavior of a convention of ministers. In both cases the members feel a sense of belongingness, affirmation and support. They affirm this cohesion by dressing, speaking, acting like each other.

The ideal goal of a church would be to achieve a sense of belonging that transcended these man-made divisions marked by appearance and dress code; where the belongingness is derived not from similar appearance, social status, or reputation, but from the common need for confession and the admission of each one's limitation.

I sensed this humbling experience at the conclusion of a Sunday morning worship service in a large Catholic church in Florida. The service was conducted in a uniquely inclusive setting — ethnically, socially, and politically. The tradition at this church called for worshippers to stand at the conclusion of the service and form a circle around the perimeter of the sanctuary, holding hands. During this time a cantor started singing phrases of the Lord's Prayer. After each phrase, worshippers responded with the same notes of his phrasing. As the prayer progressed I unexpectedly began to think about my grandson who had died in an automobile accident a few months earlier. In my attempt to stifle the sobs, I didn't realize I was trembling — my left hand was shaking. To my surprise I felt a tightened grip by the person who was holding that hand. At the conclusion of the prayer I turned with tears still in my eyes to see who it was: a tall, black teenage boy with dreadlocks. He offered a quick hug, and then turned away without a word. All human differences were transcended in that moment; it was simply two human beings in need of touch and belonging.

✛ ✛ ✛

Church membership in the US was 43% in 1920. Religious fervor created by tent preachers as well as a World

War caused church membership to grow to 61% by 1960, mostly among conservative denominations. Fundamentalism prospered with the preaching and massive evangelist meetings of Billy Graham. As religious conservatism became more widespread, the population of mainline Protestant churches declined to below fifteen percent. Non-denominational or "Community Churches" were started, and they grew. They featured contemporary music, large video screens, and gymnasiums. They employed sophisticated marketing plans. Traditional denominations attempted to follow their lead with guitar players and contemporary liturgies, but attendance continued to decline. Many in smaller communities had to close their doors, or merge with other churches. A church I once served in a small Ohio town is now the meeting place of a motorcycle club.

I read the story of the man who felt lonely, guilty and desperate for companionship. He saw a church with the front doors wide open, so he walked in just as the people inside were reading "We have left undone the things we should have done, and have done those things which we should have left undone." Hearing these words, the man said to himself, "Now I have found my kind of people." The authentically spiritual church is not a gathering of saints, but a sanctuary for sinners who have come together to accept any and all who are willing to be accepted: believer or non-believer; black or white; cranky or kind; fat or thin; rich or poor.

## Notes

1 — Nuland, Sherwin. *How We Die: Reflections on the Final Chapter.* (New York, Vintage Books, a division of Random House, 1993).

2 — History.com, "Galileo is convicted of heresy, April 12, 1633."

# Chapter 9

# Audacious

*There is no salvation outside the church.*
St. Augustine of Hippo

I confess that I once reluctantly conformed to the role of evangelist, donning the vestments, standing in front of the assembly of somber faces proclaiming the Word and what it inferred about life, death, morality, heaven and hell. Such a posture is, to put it kindly, audacious, if not vainglorious. There should be a required theological course on humility. And yet, I suppose that most of those who attend a religious service expect to hear an authoritative voice that conveys a message of reassurance, comfort, hope, and affirmation, not an invitation to challenge unexplored assumptions. And so those who boldly step into the pulpit attempt to give the devout assembly what they want to hear, which may not necessarily be what they need to hear.

## Christianity, Judaism, Islam

Does it seem irrational that religious conviction is one of the most divisive human influences? "Men never do violence so completely and cheerfully as when they do it from religious conviction." (Pascale) The Protestant Bible says, "Faith, hope, and love abide; these three. But the greatest of these is love." Yet thousands died in the war between Protestants and Catholics. The Crusades, the Inquisition, 9/11, the Middle East conflicts have all claimed thousands of lives in the name of some brand of religious conviction.

Critics of Christianity point to the violent behavior prescribed in the Bible. The Christian Bible can be perplexing to someone who might read it for the first time. Some verses approve of genocide and recommend the stoning of insubordinate children. The God of the Old Testament is neither patient nor kind. His laws are rigid. He requires that adulterers and homosexuals be put to death. The same goes for anyone who curses his parents or neglects to pray on the Day of Atonement. Muslim critics point to this biblical violence as a moral weakness of Christianity.

A strange story in the book of Judges illustrates the point, particularly in this #metoo era. As told in the nineteenth chapter of the book of Judges, a Levite (member of the Hebrew tribe of Levi) traveled to Bethlehem to secure a mistress (concubine). He packed her up and returned to his home in the remote hill country. This primitive environment did not appeal to a city girl from Bethlehem; she grew dissatisfied and escaped, returning to her father's house. After four months the Levite discovered where she had gone and went to "speak tenderly to her" and entice her to go back to his home.

For several days a negotiation took place between the Levite and the woman's father, with no apparent input from the woman herself. Each time the Levite prepared to leave, the girl's father invited him to stay another night, and then another. Finally the Levite had enough of it. He saddled up his two donkeys, took his mistress and, even though it was late in the day, he set out to return to his home in the hills.

Along the journey home he passed through the village of Gibeah, where he decided to spend the night camped out in the village square. An old man, who was coming out of the field where he had been working, took pity on the Levite and invited him and his concubine to spend the night at his house. The old man provided fodder for the donkeys and set out a table for his guests with food and wine.

Here the story takes a brutal turn. It describes an event of misogyny, rape, murder, and dismemberment that is carefully avoided in most Bible studies:

*While they were enjoying themselves, some of the wicked men of the city surrounded the house. Pounding on the door, they* shouted to the old man who owned the house, "Bring out the man who came to your house so we can have sex with him."

The owner of the house went outside and said to them, "No, my friends don't be so vile. Since this man is my guest, don't do this outrageous thing. Look, here is my virgin daughter, and his concubine. I will bring them out to you now, and you can use them and do to them whatever you wish. But as for this man, don't do such an outrageous thing."

But the men would not listen to him. So the man took his concubine and sent her outside to them, and they raped her and abused her throughout the night, and at dawn they let her go. At daybreak the woman went back to the house where her master was staying, fell down at the door and lay there until daylight.

When her master got up in the morning and opened the door of the house and stepped out to continue on his way, there lay his concubine, fallen in the doorway of the house, with her hands on the threshold. He said to her, "Get up; let's go." But there was no answer. Then the man put her on his donkey and set out for home.

When he reached home, he took a knife and cut up his concubine, limb by limb, into twelve parts and sent them into all the areas of Israel. Everyone who saw it was saying to one another, "Such a thing has never been seen or done, not since the day the Israelites came up out of Egypt. Just imagine! We must do something! So speak up!" (Judges 19:22-30).

This event reveals the primitive, barbaric culture of much early Hebrew history. Especially noteworthy is low regard these verses show for women. Paul, who was most responsible for spreading the word about Jesus to the masses, was a pious Jew. Yet Paul did not have an enlightened attitude toward women. He promoted abstinence from sex, but said if a man could not exercise self-control, he should get married, as it is "better to marry than to burn" with passion. The subtle intimation being that the woman should always be available for satisfaction of the male sexual appetite.

When we unearth some of the tawdry details of biblical literature, it cautions us to be more discerning in our judgment of other creeds and cultures. Skepticism opens ours eyes to blemishes in our own traditions. It enables us to be less judgmental toward non-Christian writings.

## Who Was This Itinerant Jewish Rabbi?

Islamic writings have a number of similarities to Christianity. Muslims teach that Jesus was born of a virgin, that he was the Messiah, and that he is the 'Word of God.' The Quran speaks of Jesus with reverence as a *witness*, a *sign*, a *mercy*, even as *the Christ of God*. Mary is revered as the mother of Jesus and is named some 34 times in the Muslim scripture, in contrast to the nineteen times mentioned in the New Testament. The doctrinal differences between the two religions grew out of their respective cultural environments. Islamic doctrine reacted against the worship of multiple gods. Therefore they rejected the Trinitarian concept of God (Father, Son, and Holy Spirit), which, admittedly, has no biblical foundation and was not defended in the early church until the third century. Islamic believers interpreted this doctrine as a continuation of polytheism.

Bible students have asked, "How many decades after his crucifixion was Jesus declared to be of equal divinity with God? How was he any different from other Old Testament references to individuals who also were referred to as God's son?" (The Lord said, you are my Son" — Psalm 2:7.) Those questions were resolved by creating the Trinitarian doctrine defined by the early church father Tertullian. At the time that he advanced the doctrine, he admitted that the majority of believers in his day did not agree with it and held more in common with Islamic teaching about who Jesus was.

It was not easy to defend the claim that Jesus' divinity was equivalent to a creator God. Was he both human and God on earth in the flesh? If he was the divine Son of God, why did he choose to appear in the flesh at that particular point in history? And why doesn't he continue to affirm his mission and divinity by appearing again from time to time — in the flesh? Did those who heard his voice and saw him in person have an advantage over us, who must rely on faith and the written word to affirm the prominence of his place in history? Later Christian scholars stated the opposite: seeing Jesus in the flesh supported the claim of his appearance as a common man, but made it more difficult to accept his divinity.

These and other questions have been debated by seekers of the truth for centuries, even though they may not disturb many unquestioning church members. As everything else changes, we want to grasp an authority that "changes not." We crave assurance. We want to know that we are right and that our connection to "rightness" is validated by an infallible source. That source is the accumulation of historical myth developed over decades of debate and speculation. The result can be a reckless trafficking in shallow religious ideas, which are exempt from theological depth.

I attended the Sunday morning service of a rapidly growing church in Florida where the pastor ended the service admonishing the members to stand and greet one another with the exclamation "Wow God!" I cringed and bowed my head in embarrassment as men and women approached me, a guest in their sanctuary, with that exclamation, so out-of-character in a worship setting.

I was raised with a fear of uttering the name "God," except in reverence. That three-letter appellation pointed toward a mysterious and transcendent power. Today, it has become commonly used to describe every emotion from derision to surprise: "goddamn you" or OMG!

A Catholic Church in rural Ohio was vandalized with spray paint. Across the front of the church in large letters were the words "God's Not Real!!" Such irreverent graffiti should not surprise us, considering the conflicted message conveyed from the pulpit to the work place.

Where is the *gravitas,* the mystery, the supremacy of an almighty when we reduce the omnipotent **I Am Who I Am** to a chant, an exclamation, or a talisman? In the earliest years of biblical revelation, the name of God was regarded with such awe that it could not be spoken or even written. The second commandment admonishes "You shall not take the name of the Lord your God in vain." Martin

Luther explained that this commandment means we should not "curse, swear, lie or deceive, but call on him in prayer, praise, and thanksgiving." To some sensitive ears, cursing sounds abrasive, almost like defiling one's family name.

✚ ✚ ✚

After Jesus' death, stories began to circulate about his teaching. In order to give his message ascendant authority and impress others to convert to the new religion, Jesus was called "Son of God," a title used in both the Old and New Testaments to refer to those with a special relationship to God. In the Old Testament pious men and Kings of Israel are called sons of God. In the New Testament Adam is called son of God (Luke 3:38).

During the three decades following Jesus' crucifixion, it was believed that Jesus was a great prophet, a Messiah. This was accepted by the major oriental religions — Jews and Muslims. But the claim of divinity had not yet been made. There were no "Christians" yet. This term arose at least three decades after the crucifixion, as recorded in Acts 11: 26: "and the disciples were first called Christians in Antioch."

Like Judaism, Jesus was not considered to be on the same level of divinity in Islamic teaching. He was not God. Islamic literature proclaimed that there is only One God. This teaching was a reaction to the polytheism, the idol worship of Arabic culture. Likewise in Jewish theology, the Messiah was considered a human being chosen and blessed by God, not God in the flesh. Jewish theology teaches that as the Messiah, he was the ultimate culmination of prophecy.

Early theologians took great pains to find the right wording for a trinitarian description of God — a unity in three parts. The doctrine of the Trinity is not a biblical construct. As mentioned earlier, it became a theological formula in the third century when it was defined in the writings of Tertullian, in which God is described as Father, Son, and Holy Spirit. It was in those New Testament writings, recorded decades after Jesus died, that attempts were made to elevate Jesus to divine status. He became more than the human

Messiah, the greatest of all prophets. Gradually he became God himself. These bold claims gave a loftier credence to the newly founded religion.

The earliest New Testament writings are more congruent with Jewish and Islamic theology than are those New Testament books written at a later date. The book of James is considered by many biblical scholars to be the first recorded New Testament book, written sometime after 60 CE or three decades after Jesus' crucifixion. James, the brother of Jesus, was a pious Jew who emphasized the importance of the Jewish Law as the manifestation of faith. He mentions Jesus Christ only twice, and makes no reference to the resurrection or to Jesus being a source of redemption. Like Islam, the biblical book of James emphasizes the theology of one god (not a Trinity), describes the importance of good deeds, and makes no reference to the Holy Spirit or the divinity of Christ.

*What is it, my brethren, if a man says he has faith, but he has no works? Can that faith save him?...Even so, faith, if it has no works, is dead, being by itself...are you willing to recognize, you foolish fellow, that faith without works is useless?...You see that a man is justified by works, and not by faith alone...For just as the body without the spirit is dead, so also faith without works is dead.* (Selected verses from James 2:14-26).

This doctrine espoused by James was challenged by the teachings of Paul.

## The Man From Tarsus

Paul's parents, wealthy merchants from the city of Tarsus, wanted their son to become a rabbi. They sent him to study with Gamaliel, the grand Pharisee teacher of Jerusalem. Until Paul started preaching the message about Jesus to the Gentiles, forty years after the crucifixion, every believer was Jewish. The pillars of the early church, James, Peter, and John, were stalwart Jews. The fact that Christians throughout history ever participated in anti-Semitism, shows either ignorance or denial of their nascent history.

In contrast to the writings of the book of James, Paul repeatedly claims that good works have nothing to do with salvation doctrine. The Pauline doctrine became the core of Martin Luther's theology:

*Therefore having been justified by faith, we have peace with God through our Lord Jesus Christ...For while we were still helpless, at the right time Christ died for the ungodly...But God demonstrates his own love toward us, in that while we were yet sinners, Christ died for us. Much more then, having now been justified by his blood, we shall be saved from the wrath of God through him...So then as through one transgression there resulted condemnation to all men, even so through one act of righteousness there resulted justification of life to all men...but where sin increased, grace abounded all the more.* (from Romans 5:1-20).

It was from this Pauline letter to the Romans that Martin Luther drew his core teaching of *sola fide*, faith alone; human behavior is not the determining factor in spiritual salvation. Is it any wonder that Martin Luther called the Letter of James "an epistle of straw?" Luther didn't think it should be included in the New Testament, despite the claim of many scholars that it was the earliest recorded canonical writing following Jesus' death. For Paul, and later for Martin Luther, radical grace became the singularly distinctive Christian maxim. Redemption is not based on human behavior, but is purely a gift of faith. This became the cardinal doctrine of the Protestant Reformation — *sola fide*, by faith alone.

Paul carries it further. He says "...where sin increased, grace increased all the more." What? The more we sin, the more we are forgiven? That can be carried to ridiculous limits. So Paul realizes the potential misunderstanding of that claim and qualifies it with the question: "What shall we say, then? Shall we go on sinning so that grace may increase? By no means!" (Romans 6:1-2).

This Protestant doctrine has been often challenged. Where do you draw the line at too much sinfulness to qualify for forgiveness and salvation? Paul, and the Protestant theologians who interpret his message, say there is no line.

Salvation is promised to the most egregious sinner if he or she turns to find refuge in God's love.

> *For I am convinced that neither death, nor life, nor angels, nor principalities, nor things present, nor things to come, nor powers, nor height, nor depth, nor any other created thing, shall be able to separate us from the love of God, which is in Christ Jesus our Lord."* (Romans 8:38-39).

This passage has brought comfort to many a sensitive conscience. It has relieved the hearts of thousands who have come to believe that they are beyond hope; it includes all the reprobates who have ever come to believe they are worthless.

Does the Easter message give any credit for our good deeds, our patience toward a nasty neighbor, our kindness to the poor? What about that self-assuring claim that, 'I pray every day, I tithe, I forgive my co-worker for stealing from me? Does that bring us closer to redemption?' Not really. Jesus said, "I have not come to call the righteous, but sinners" (Mark 2:17).

Are some sinners more worthy of the calling than others? That is how the law of human justice works, in which there are degrees of corrupt and fraudulent activity, some requiring greater punishment than others. But Paul doesn't draw that line. "Christ died for the ungodly...while we were yet sinners..." And furthermore, 'all have sinned and fallen short.'

Is it any wonder that this radical message was mocked and ridiculed, its earliest missionaries martyred for promoting this doctrine? It's bound to rub folks the wrong way. The ones who embraced it most eagerly were the outcasts, the lowlifes, the drifters.

After centuries of watering down the radical implication of this doctrine, it became endorsed by secular rulers and spread among the masses. Ultimately it was culturally accepted, and enhanced with stained glass windows, incense, elegant liturgies, and impressive temples, which often served more as a symbol of the power of the sovereign ruler than a glorification of a god.

The testimony of Jesus' brother, James, namely, that good behavior IS a necessary qualification, never completely went away, especially in Roman Catholic doctrine. This became a primary sticking point between Martin Luther and the Roman Catholic Church during the Reformation. "What use is it for a man to say he has faith when he does nothing to show it? Can that faith save him?" In other words, a certain amount of "conversion" has to take place, showing evidence that "faith" is legitimized by ethical behavior (James 2:14). In fact the greatest impetus to the spread of this new religion was the fact that its devotees took seriously the gospel instruction to practice compassion, to care for the sick, to feed the hungry, to clothe the poor. This was carried out not only among their own members, but extended to anyone, friend or foe.

This is the point illustrated by Jesus' parable of the Good Samaritan: a Jewish citizen was attacked and left to die by the side of the road. Two religious leaders go by and decide not to get involved. Then along comes a Samaritan, whom Jews viewed as half-breeds. Jews and Samaritans hated each other. It is this Samaritan who, though he knew the wounded man hated him and would mistreat him if he had a chance, takes pity on him. He goes to him and bandages his wounds, pouring on oil and wine. Then he puts the man on his own donkey, takes him to an inn and pays to have him cared for (Luke 10:33-34). This kind of radical love was something new in a society where people of different cultures and colors were expected to despise each other. It was a message that resounded loudly enough to spread rapidly and overcome a culture where prejudice and cruelty existed.

Is it not fair to say that in civilized cultures today, justice can be measured by how it treats its most vulnerable members? Civilized countries attempt to promote and maintain a higher level of compassion and acknowledge the value of all human life.

The Gospels — Matthew, Mark, Luke, John — and Epistles of Saint Paul were written later — a decade or so after the book of James. Were Matthew, Mark, Luke, and John the authors of those gospels? No, the writers of those gospels were not the original disciples. They were scribes who recorded what had become oral tradition, such as stories that were passed on person-to-person, or recited in spiritual gatherings, until they were finally written down. It was common practice for authors to title their writings according to the teacher from whom the writings had descended through oral tradition. The original disciples of Jesus eventually had their own followers, some of whom were scribes who recorded the teachings. The disciples themselves, while they may have been teachers, were not the writers of the gospels ascribed to their names. None of those who actually put the gospels in writing had ever seen Jesus, just as Paul never saw or heard Jesus' own voice.

Today we often refer to "the gospel of Matthew," or "the gospel of Luke." But in the original Greek, they were called "the gospel *according to* Matthew," or "the gospel *according to* Luke." Ascribing these teachings to an original disciple, even though they were actually written by those who had never seen or heard Jesus, gave them authenticity. This was common practice among early writers and was not considered to be plagiarism or pedantry.

The earliest written gospel was the gospel according to Saint Mark. It was written after the fall of the second temple, which occurred in 70 AD. It forms the core of what is called the synoptic gospels (Matthew, Mark, and Luke); 76% of the verses in Mark are reproduced almost word for word in both Matthew and Luke. Matthew contains 606 of Mark's 661 verses.

The writer of Mark's gospel does not claim to be an eye-witness to Jesus' ministry. He uses various sources, including a narrative that had circulated for several decades. This story, which had been passed around orally, described the final period in the life of Jesus, covering his entrance to Jerusalem and leading to his crucifixion on Mount Calvary. This first-written gospel also includes collections of miracle stories (oral or written), teachings about the final destruction of the world, and moral instructions. These stories were in circulation year after year, repeated in different languages and in countries other than where Jesus lived and taught. As they evolved, they were enhanced and in some cases exaggerated. At each telling the message accumulated more detail as it was spread by word from one teacher to the next. Understandably, it would be misleading to think that Jesus' actual words are recorded in these documents, because they were not written until thirty and forty years after they were spoken.

This understanding of biblical history is something that evangelical ministers learn during their first year in seminary. It is New Testament 101. The more seriously you and I take biblical scripture, the more we want to know its history — how it was written, when it was written, and how it related to its cultural environment. Some clergy may avoid sharing this deeper study of scripture because of a concern that it could undermine the shaky faith of some in their congregation. One should never underestimate the intellectual and spiritual capacity of those worshiping in the church pews.

After many years of witnessing a sort of hero worship of Jesus, I discovered the Gnostic writings that modified my understanding of corporate worship. I admit with a sense of guilt that the spaces between my Sunday church attendances have grown wider. Lodged in my conscience is the unspoken assumption, inculcated from the earliest years of upbringing, that in our culture good people go to church. It becomes part of one's life experience, and if you try to ignore it or avoid it, a nagging guilt haunts you for the rest of the day, especially if you grew up with this habitual practice.

There are abundant reasons to encourage the practice of worship: people who attend church regularly are statistically healthier and live longer; learning the biblical stories, myths, history is part of the educational process and without it we would miss out on a significant body of knowledge; we mingle with caring people in churches, which inspires benevolence and healthy social interaction. (Sammy asks his father, "Why do you go to church, daddy. I didn't think you believed in God the way Mr. Johnson does." His father says, "It's like this, Sammy. Johnson goes to church to talk to God. I go to church to talk to Johnson.")

Despite my respect for the historical church, which founded most of our hospitals and early institutions of higher learning, I started to find the Sunday morning service unfulfilling, and the sermons even a little depressing. Many seemed shallow in theology, simplistic in their application; often a linear exegesis of the Bible verses that had been read earlier in the service; or a theatrical performance by a frustrated actor. The part of the Sunday morning service that brought the most inspiration was the organ prelude, the message and inspiration of the hymns, the sights and voices of small children, and the moments of silence. These moments were too rare within the sixty minute discipline of sitting sedately in a church pew. Much of what I witnessed took on the appearance of a performance: amateur singers enjoying their moment on the stage, and testimonials about dramatic conversions from a life of sin to salvation. On occasion I heard a sermon that was provocative, challenging, and intellectually stimulating.

I agree with the early American minister Ralph Waldo Emerson when he wrote, "I once heard a preacher who sorely tempted me to say I would go to church no more...He had not one word intimating that he had laughed or wept, was married or in love, had been commended, or cheated, or chagrined...The true preacher can be known by this, that he deals out to the people his life, life passed through the fire of thought."[1]

I don't want to hear an egotistical rehearsal of the preacher's life, but I *am* interested if the minister can explain how he may have solved a serious dilemma through the intervention of biblical insight or divine inspiration.

✠ ✠ ✠

One day I walked into the Gulfport, Florida, library and found a shelf with several books about the Gnostic gospels. I took one off the shelf, sat down in a library chair, and found myself lost in fascination for the next few hours. The thirteen leather-bound codices, which constitute the discovery of Gnostic gospels, contain over fifty texts and were discovered in Egypt in 1945. They had been hidden away for centuries in a cave. Many were so brittle from age that it took several years to chemically treat them so they could be translated by scholars at Princeton and Harvard. They revealed that early Christianity included dozens of gospels, not just the four that are in our Bible.

Why had they been hidden? It is a story which hints at an important time of intrigue in the establishment of the early church. These writings taught that there was an inner connection between humanity and God, which did not require any outside intervention. Ecclesiastical leaders were in the process of creating a formula which required priestly intervention for access to divine grace and forgiveness. To allow the promulgation of this kind of unmediated salvation would interfere with the advancement of an institutional religion, i.e. a church. The message in these Gnostic writings is an indication of how political influences were at work in the formation of the early church and the selection of what would be included in the Bible as well as what would be rejected.

One of those Gnostic gospels, the Gospel of Thomas, which is an early record of Jesus' sayings, encourages the hearer not so much to believe in Jesus, as to seek to know God through one's own, divinely inherent capacity, since we all are created in the image of God. This could not be tolerated while the church hierarchy was becoming formally organized in the fourth century. Church leaders had to emphasize the singular spiritual impotence of individuals and the consequent necessity of an ecclesiastical intermediary. This meant endorsing only those writings which supported a hierarchical authority, and dismissing those which did not. It would not do to have scriptural writings which put a higher value on a believer's access to grace without an intermediary, omitting the necessity of an ecclesiastically-ordained authority.

The Gnostic doctrine reveals the influence of Eastern mystical orientation of Hinduism, considered to be the world's oldest religion. Jesus was undoubtedly familiar with these Hindu teachings, which originated hundreds of years before his birth and were commonly known and practiced in his culture.

Gnostic teachings challenged adherents to discover what lies hidden within us, as the means to commune with God. This abnegates the necessity of ecclesiastical intervention. Such instruction would obviously not be helpful to clerics and bishops who were dedicating themselves to the establishment of an official religious order in which the word and sacrament (external sources) would be officially administered. Gnosticism taught that you will find the true relationship with God only within yourself, not through the mediation of a separate individual or church body. You must search for it with a pure mind. Only then will you attain ultimate enlightenment. Ignore this interior gift at your own risk.

Stephan Hoeller writes in his book, *Jung and the Lost Gospels*:[2] "In every soul there is a hunger for that kind of direct vision that bestows wholeness and true meaning. Unless we know how to deal creatively with this hunger, it projects itself outward, independently of our will, even against our will, usually upon an unsuitable object...Only consciousness, engendered by Gnosis, can prevent the living out of false projections and the consequent violence and cruelty."

Proof of this claim is seen in the violence of organized religious factions which grasp onto the certitude of an institutional creed. It has given rise to divisiveness, hatred, and war — Protestant against Catholic, against Jew, against Muslim.

The earliest founders of the church were asking themselves, how can we possibly establish an institution, require its members to attend the services, and motivate them to provide financial support, unless we teach that it is the only way to attain eternal life? The rituals of baptism, word and sacrament must become essential elements of humanity's relationship to God. And the divine message must be pronounced through the mediation of appointed disciples — priests and ministers, all ordained to a holy calling.

In 367 AD a bishop named Athanasius demanded that Egyptian monks destroy all religious writings except those that he listed as "acceptable." These writings became the early core for what we call The New Testament. Rather than inviting the authors of other (Gnostic) gospels into a conference for discussion and mutual enlightenment, Athanasius and his cohorts condemned the authors as the anti-Christ and the agents of Satan. Enlightenment, they proclaimed, could be attained only through the church, which administered the "means of salvation," such as the sacraments.

Too bad for history! Maybe a more open minded reflection could have prevented some of the bloodshed of martyrs, or the so-called "Holy Wars," in which thousands were murdered for their opposing beliefs. The richness of the early decades of Christian thought existed in the diversity of beliefs. There were dozens of gospels, beautifully written, thoughtfully articulate, deeply spiritual. In one of them Jesus is quoted as saying, "If you bring forth what is within you, what you do not bring forth will destroy you." The challenge was to discover what lies hidden within as a means to commune with God. But this did not serve the purpose of establishing an institution. These alien theologians would have to be annihilated, rather than invited into their circle for debate and discussion.

Call it divine intervention or scholarly disobedience, but one of the monks, maybe with a few close friends, sneaked the forbidden books, which Athanasius wanted burned, out of the monastery, sealed them in six foot high earthenware crocks and buried them in a cave in the Nag Hammadi, Egypt. It would take sixteen hundred years before a humble sheep herder would stumble across them when he went inside to find shelter from the burning sun.

## Notes

1 — Emerson, Ralph Waldo. *Nature and Selected Essays.* (New York, Viking Penguin, Inc. 1982) p. 118.

2 — Hoeller, Stephan. *Jung and the Lost Gospels: Insights into the Dead Sea Scrolls and the Nag Hammadi Library.* (Wheaton, Illinois, Quest Books. 1989).

# Chapter 10

# A Discovery That Changed History

*A book is not harmless merely because no one is consciously offended by it.*
    T.S. Eliot

In December 1945, an Arab peasant was digging around a massive boulder in Egypt. He hit a red earthenware jar almost as tall as he was. He was excited by his find and thought it might contain gold, so he smashed the jar and discovered fourteen papyrus books bound in leather. They contained 52 texts of various gospels which had a different message from the existing Christian tradition. He figured they might be valuable, so he took them home and hid them in straw bales by the fireplace. He forgot to tell his mother. When she started the cooking fire, she used the straw and some of the papyrus to kindle the flame. Fortunately, most of the books were saved and sold to an antiquities dealer in Cairo. Eleven of the thirteen leather bound volumes (each of which contained several books) ended up in a museum in Cairo, Egypt. They eventually found their way to the United States, through the deciphering labor of Professor Gilles Quispel, distinguished professor of religion at Utrecht, in the Netherlands. They became referred to as the Gnostic Gospels. The meaning of gnostic and Gnosticism deserves more attention than I give it here. These writings reveal the startling message, "these are the secret words which the living Jesus spoke, and which the twin, Judas Thomas, wrote down."

Curious students of biblical history should read one of Elaine Pagles books, which include *The Gnostic Gospels* and *Beyond Belief: the Secret Gospel of Thomas*. A professor at Princeton Theological Seminary, she spent many years studying these ancient gnostic writings, which preceded the writing of the biblical gospels, Matthew, Mark, Luke, and John. The content of these 52 books from the earliest centuries of Christianity is astonishing. Suddenly we find out that there were not just four gospels. In fact dozens of gospels had been written. What made these findings valuable was that they were all undoubtedly in circulation before any of our four gospels were written. These earlier Christian writings represented a wide range of insights about who Jesus was, what he taught, and how Christians should respond.

Those gospels, discovered in our lifetime, had titles such as Gospel of Thomas, Gospel of Mary, Gospel of Truth, Gospel to the Egyptians, Apocalypse of Paul. Many of these gospels were written by a sect called Christian Gnostics, who claimed to possess a revealed knowledge (*gnosis* in Greek) that led to a closer relationship with God.

One of the most impressive of these writings was the Gospel of Thomas, which contained many of the earliest sayings of Jesus. The message of these early sayings of Jesus was that when we learn to know ourselves at the deepest level we will know God. Expressed in non-religious language, it meant that dedicated reflection could reveal our connection to a higher nature.

This is vastly different from our traditional religious view, which insists that a vast chasm separates humanity from a creator; that God is entirely separate and wholly other from mankind. The Gnostic gospels claimed that because we are made in the image of God, our knowledge of this higher power is revealed through self-knowledge.

Consider for a moment where this might lead if one was attempting to establish an institution. The practice of faith becomes a matter of reflection, meditation, and soul searching. *For what reason were you born? How can you discover who you were meant to be? How are you able to relate to your spouse, your children? Who are you in relation to your neighbors, your community? What do your failures teach you? Where can you discover peace and contentment? Are you more than flesh and blood and animal instinct?* Gnosticism teaches you to meditate until the answers emerge.

It is important to ask, "Why were these gospel writings hidden away? And why were they considered to be heresy?"

By now the answer may seem obvious. These books were abandoned at a time when the church was becoming established as an institution led by bishops, priests, and deacons, who understood that their mission was to preserve the one "true faith." This true faith was the possession of the church. Outside that church there could be no salvation. Whoever challenged that view was denounced as a heretic and was excommunicated.

Early ecclesiastical leaders rejected these Gnostic teachings in order to establish and protect an institutional organization. They had to develop a message which upheld their own influence and the influence of institutional religion. Anything contrary to this had to be rejected and labeled as heresy. How could one gain loyalty to a religious institution if the practice of faith was a matter of personal meditation and intellectual discovery?

Those Gnostic writings, discovered over seventy years ago in that earthen jar, did not support the idea of an institutional church under the leadership of chosen ministers. In the gospel of Thomas, Jesus is quoted as saying, "If you bring forth what is within you, what you bring forth will save you. If you do not bring forth what is within you, what you do not bring forth will destroy you." According to the gospel of Thomas, Jesus rebuked those who sought access to God elsewhere.

But this would never do for those who were trying to build an institution upon which every person must be dependent for his spiritual wellbeing. How could you teach that ecclesiastical intervention was the only path to God and salvation, when these teachings were promoting a theology that a spark of divinity dwelt within each individual; that it must be sought through *gnosis* in order to realize one's full spiritual potential? How could you entice the masses to provide financial support to an ecclesiastical organization, unless they believed that the church was essential to their salvation?

It was natural, then, that any ideas contrary to the development of institutional religion became labeled as heresy. For Christianity to succeed as an institutional religion there had to be consensus about the legitimacy of the authority of those who claimed exclusive leadership over the church as successors of the apostles.

Gnosticism was a fascinating discovery for me. It increased my ambition to continue the search for truth. It threw up a warning to beware of gullibility or easy acceptance of certitude when searching for answers to spiritual questions. Even convictions that have stood for centuries can turn out to be false.

This information did not diminish my appreciation for the church. I was raised in the church and became one of its ministers. Growing up in a family that taught the importance of church attendance endowed me with a discipline in the values of compassion, humility, and faith in the potential goodness of the universe. Worship, prayer, and study of scriptures grounded me in the elements of our Judeo-Christian culture. The psalms, the sayings of Jesus, the instructions of Saint Paul come back to the forefront of my mind for guidance in times of celebration as well as times of grief and despair. The three years of catechism beginning when I was twelve years old gave me a foundation upon which to evaluate the creeds and principles of other belief systems. It stretched my mind to memorize the titles of the 66 books of the Bible, the Creeds, the Ten Commandments, and prayers of the church, as well as Luther's explanations to each of these. This large body of information had to be committed to memory.

I chuckled when I watched a video of Jay Leno's random interviews with university students. He asked each of them to name one of the Ten Commandments. None of them could name a single commandment. One student guessed, "Freedom of speech?"

After viewing this illiteracy, I am thankful for the strict catechetical discipline, against which I rebelled at the time. It saved me from having to admit ignorance of the most significant set of guidelines ever revealed in the history of human culture.

At the time I was not happy about having to spend hours memorizing dozens of pages. Now I am grateful for those who pushed and prodded me to stretch my memory, and prepare my spirit for life's dissensions and protests, as well as life's advantages and opportunities.

As I reflect on who has most positively influenced my life, I realize it has not been the easy lessons, the tender-hearted teachers who have molded the raw material of character. Rather it was the teachers whose classes I dreaded attending at times; the piano instructors who left me in tears; the words from parents and superiors that stung at the time they were directed at me. Without these I would be someone who gave up too easily, who shied away from challenges that appeared too difficult, and who thought I deserved special favors and attention.

I have learned to accept the fact that the church is a humanly conceived institution. It has been responsible for many cultural achievements — hospitals, universities, and organizations to care for the needy. It has provided a community of common values with which I could become a part. Therefore I support it as I would any other valuable human institution.

Unfortunately, it has also at times caused division and bloodshed. It is fully imbued with human nature and the egos of its leaders. It has gone through difficult periods of history its leadership has damaged its reputation. But my discovery of Gnosticism did not prejudice my faith in the church. Rather it stretched my faith in the revelation of a possible omnipotence that is far above any human institution, and that might be available to everyone, without intervention.

Despite its human limitations and periods of disrepute, the historical church has been central to the development of American moral culture. The American Revolution was based on a belief in the sovereign authority of God, in contrast to the French revolution, which was founded on the sovereignty of man. John Adams wrote in 1798, "Our constitution was made only for a moral and religious people. It is wholly inadequate to the government of any other." And, at least at this point in history, the church is a valid teaching institution to convey ethical and moral precepts that are necessary for civilization to survive.

## The New Testament And The Formation Of The Church

By the end of the first century there were many gospels circulating, in addition to the four with which we are familiar. By 200 AD, Christianity was becoming an established institutional structure with bishops, priests, and deacons. They assumed the position of guardians of the only "true faith." In order to protect their status they denounced as heresy all other viewpoints that did not recognize the one church, outside of which there was no salvation. In other words, they had to weed out and condemn any writings that did not support their authority as the protectors of the established church.

The content of the New Testament was not finally determined until 350 years after Christ. The Synod of Laodicea established the first official determination of the New Testament in 350 AD. The members of that council voted to include the four gospels, the Acts of the Apostles, the seven Catholic Epistles (James, 1 & 2 Peter, 1,2,3 John, Jude) and the 14 epistles of Paul, including Hebrews. The book of Revelation was not mentioned. Seventeen years later, Saint Athanasius set the book of Revelation alongside the other 26 books previously approved. However, the authenticity of the book of Hebrews and the book of Revelation continued to be contested in later years. Martin Luther never accepted the book of Revelation as having a legitimate place in the Bible.

✠ ✠ ✠

It is evident that the Bible is an important historical document with which any enlightened person should be familiar. It contains information that has ethical and historical value. Some of the writings can be said to have been inspired by higher understanding of human nature. Some biblical stories simply record legends and oral history that had circulated among Hebrew and Arabic tribes for decades before they were recorded on papyrus. In any case the heavy hand of human authority is evident in determining the final content of our Bible.

# Chapter 11

# Ecclesiastical Humor — Censored

*A bitter jest, when it comes too near the truth, leaves a sharp sting behind it.*
Publius Cornelius Tacitus, d. 117 AD

My Puritan sensibilities surface when I learn that someone I had assumed was morally beyond reproach reveals a surprising degree of male libido. I should remind myself of the earthy humor once shared among theologians and church leaders when they met at conventions. Some of the most indelicate humor I have heard was told by theology professors and high ranking ecclesiastical dignitaries.

However, there have been periods of history when bawdy humor reflected a base immorality among religious as well as secular leaders. In *The Swerve* Harvard Professor Stephen Greenblatt describes in extensive detail the sixteenth century period of history, which was rife with ecclesiastical corruption as well as criminal acts of moral atrocity. The priesthood was often a pathway into a life of depravity. Priests amassed great wealth by exploiting the weaknesses of the peasants. Those who became priests could anticipate a life of food and drink served by young boys. Mistresses and courtesans were available to entertain the deacons and priests, offering such entertainment as lewd songs, naked breasts, and fondling, all for a modest price.

I preface this with a *mea culpa* for including some of the uncouth language that appears in the next few paragraphs, as well as the revelations about famous theologian Paul Tillich.

"A good f--- can make even an agnostic see God."[1] K.D.West (See the exculpatory note at the end of this chapter.)

✠ ✠ ✠

In the winter of 1417, an unemployed Italian secretary to the pope, Poggio Bracciolini, was nosing around the remote corners of a monastery in southern Germany in search of ancient manuscripts. He was a brilliant scholar who loved books. He had already hunted through most of the monastic libraries in Italy, where he had hung out with papal advisories and dignitaries.

Poggio enjoyed being at the center of what he called "the Bugiale," the Lie Factory in the Vatican. This was a room where the papal secretaries gathered to exchange jokes and stories. Over the course of serving seven different popes, he had documented these stories and conversations in a volume he entitled the *Facetiae*. Most of the stories in this collection are about sex, as well as the ignorance and greed of the Vatican priests. One joke is about a Cardinal boss who demands a corrected rewriting of a document. The scribal secretary brings back an identical document, pretending that he has changed it. The Cardinal ostentatiously appears to review it and, although it is the same as the original, he pronounces that it is now correct.

If one is curious, the *Facetiae* can be found on Google, digitized from an 1879 publication containing both the Latin and English translation.

One of the stories is about Cardinal de' Conte, a stout and burly man. He had been out hunting, and, toward noon, feeling hungry, came down to dinner; he took his seat at table, perspiring copiously (it was summer time) and requested that someone should air him with a fan. The servants had left the room on various duties, and he asked a certain Evardo Lupi, Apostolic Secretary, to ventilate him. "But," said the latter, "I do not know how that is done with you."

"Never mind," answered the Cardinal; "do it as you like, in your own way."

"All right, by Jove," replied the Secretary, and raising his right leg, he emitted from the very depths of his bowels the most sonorous fart, saying at the same time that that was how he was accustomed to make a breeze for himself. There was a numerous company who could not help bursting out into a fit of laughter.

And this: A man who had given his wife a valuable dress, complained that he never exercised his marital rights without it costing him more than a golden ducat each time. "It is your fault," answered the wife; why do you not, by frequent repetition, bring down the cost to one farthing."

Since we have dared to stray this far from propriety, I will dare to share one more story; this one was included in *The Swerve*. It is the story of a quack doctor who says that he can produce children of different skills — generals, soldiers, merchants — depending on how far he pushes in his cock. An ignorant peasant makes a deal with the doctor to have his wife conceive a soldier. He hands her over and at the last minute jumps out of hiding and smacks the quack doctor's ass to push his cock further in. "Per Sancta Dei Evangelia," the peasant shouts triumphantly. "Hic erit Papa!" "This one is going to be Pope!"[2]

*The Swerve: How the World Became Modern,* by Stephen Greenblatt, describes a period in the church's history when the pope ruled over a large part of Italy. In order to hold onto his empire, he had to use force and treachery. There was little apparent difference between the moral code of ecclesiastical dignitaries and secular society. More of that seems to be coming to light today.

✠ ✠ ✠

The *Facetiae* was hugely popular and gained wide circulation. But with the arrival of the Protestant Reformation came the need to clean up their act; so the church condemned the *Facetiae* to be burned, along with other unacceptable works, such as those by Erasmus and Machiavelli. Poggio wrote with alarming honesty about the church and papal court in which he worked: "There is seldom room for talent or honesty; everything is obtained through intrigue or luck, not to mention money, which seems to hold supreme sway over the world." In order to restore their reputation and maintain credibility they realized that they must eradicate the subversive humor along with other critical works.

During his book search in 1417, Poggio stumbled onto one of the most momentous finds of any century. Had he known its potential to change the world of theology and philosophy, he might have destroyed it. The discovery, *De Rerum Natura,* "On the Nature of Things," had been written fifty years before Christ. It was dangerously radical and advocated in the most dramatic literary style an atheistic philosophy. Poggio ordered a scribe to make a copy. That copy was rediscovered in the 1700s. We don't know if he realized that he was releasing a book that had the potential to take down the order and structure of the church.

The two thousand year old manuscript was written by a poet and philosopher, Titus Lucretius Carus. Lucretius was a brilliant scholar of philosophy and science. His work, *De Rerum Natura,* combined the depth of his knowledge with near perfect poetic mastery.

*On the Nature of Things* was not an easy manuscript to read. But this did not discourage Poggio, who was a brilliant scholar and well-grounded in Latin. He was eager to solve the textual riddles and unveil the complex propositions. Written in the standard unrhymed six-beat lines in which Latin poets wrote their epic verses, the manuscript combined theories on religion, pleasure, and death. It plumbed the depths of the physical world, the nature of disease, the evolution of human societies, along with the dangers and joys of sex.

The Lucretian philosophy is the bible of atheistic epistemology. Lucretius claims that all organized religions are superstitious delusions. Almost all of them include the myth of the sacrifice of a child, which Lucretius believed was clear evidence of religious perversity. Because he believed in no afterlife, Lucretius proposed that life should be organized to attain the greatest pleasure and avoid pain.

The theory that pleasure is the highest good would not be a difficult doctrine to promote. It was proclaimed, however, with the stipulation that it could only be achieved if pursued prudently and honorably. The greatest obstacle to pleasure is not pain; it is delusion and uncontrolled desire. While it is reasonable to enjoy sexual pleasure, Lucretius claimed that it was a mistake to let it become all-consuming or lead to a craving desire to possess the object of that pleasure. Lucretius undoubtedly knew about the writings of a Greek philosopher who lived a couple hundred years before him. Epicurus had promoted a life style of calculated hedonism: in other words. that happiness is the highest good and is best achieved by prudently pursuing pleasure and avoiding pain. The ultimate attainment of pleasure requires discipline and a consideration of what is in one's long-term self-interest.

Lucretius understood that an insatiable sexual appetite can never be completely fulfilled. He composed one of the most erotic descriptions of sexual passion ever recorded: "Even in the hour of possession, the passion of the lovers fluctuate and wander in uncertainty: they cannot decide what to enjoy first with their eyes and hands. They tightly squeeze the object of their desire and cause bodily pain, often driving their teeth into one another's lips and crushing mouth against mouth." W.B. Yeats called this "the finest description of sexual intercourse ever written."

Poggio must have taken to heart the hedonist ethic. At age 56 he abandoned his long-time mistress, as well as the fourteen children he had produced with her, and married a girl less than 18 years old. Despite the dire warnings of his friends, because of the almost forty year age difference, it was a happy marriage, producing five sons and a daughter.

French philosopher Montaigne shared Lucretius' contempt for a morality enforced by the threat of an afterlife. He wrote, "I want death to find me planting my cabbages, but careless of death, and still more my unfinished garden."

## A Contemporary Theologian

Paul Tillich could be considered one of the most influential religious scholars of this century. He did not tolerate self-centered emotional religious affirmations that are stubbornly embraced in order to escape from emptiness and loss of meaning. He believed that unquestioning religious conviction reveals a shallow attempt to avoid deeper analysis. Rather than taking theology seriously, it follows the easier route to pathological self-delusion. We are foolish and naïve to surrender the right to doubt or ask questions. When a religious conclusion is reached without the right to question or continue searching for deeper meaning, such religion will protect and feed a potentially neurotic mentality.

While Tillich was a towering existential theologian and philosopher, he had a libertine attitude when it came to moral standards. His second wife, Hanna, wrote an autobiography about their marriage entitled *From Time to Time*[3]. Tillich was her third husband. She was erotically attracted to him, not because of his physical appearance, but because of his profound intellect. A former art student, she had engaged in affairs with men and women. She described the time a couple invited Paul and her for an evening soiree. During the evening, "a long-legged lesbian aristocrat came sailing into the room on a bicycle, wearing pink leggings, her face painted, flowers in her hair, imitating a circus beauty. The kissing, drinking, and flirting were indiscriminate. I felt uncomfortable. Paul was delighted."

Tillich's brilliant intellectual capacity challenges a reader of his theological writings. In his book *The Courage to Be*[4], Tillich writes that we live in an "age of anxiety." One of the sources of this anxiety is our limited life span. We seek relief from our emptiness, from the element of doubt, which is a "condition of all spiritual life," by hanging on to what we already know and understand, or what others in our closest relationships affirm as fact. We cling to traditions, convictions and emotional preferences. We lose our spiritual center and question the meaning of our existence. We try to find escape from our emptiness but nothing satisfies.

Tillich is critical of our modern interpretations of faith. The concept of faith "has lost its genuine meaning and has received the connotation of 'belief in something unbelievable.'" We should not try to analyze or define our faith.

"Simply accept the fact that you are accepted! In that moment, grace conquers sin." Nothing is demanded but acceptance, to "accept oneself as accepted in spite of being unacceptable."

We try to make God accessible by portraying Him in a symbol or a verse of scripture. But the more concrete we are about that image of God, the more elusive God is. The closer we get to that god, the further we are from the reality of God, who is beyond description or definition.

We come closest to God when we surrender all intellectual concepts. And then, at our very lowest, when our ego has evaporated, we may be touched by a 'stroke of grace,' and experience the revelation that although "I am dust and ashes, though I am nothing, yet I am something through a God who created and accepts me."

There are parallels with the theology of an earlier German, Martin Luther, who made this discovery after trying again and again to eliminate pride and to become worthy of God's love. He finally concluded that it was impossible. Sinful pride was inherent in every motivation to be good, to be worthy, to be acceptable to God. After days and nights of emotional struggle, even painful self-flagellation, Luther, with inspiration from his study of the writings of Saint Paul, came to the realization that there is nothing anyone can do to deserve God's grace. "For all have sinned and fall short of the glory of God, and are justified freely by his grace... For we maintain that a man is justified by faith apart from observing the law" (Romans 3:23, 28). There is nothing we can do to make God love us. There is nothing we can do to make God stop loving us.

Tillich says that we deceive ourselves if we flee from the pain of emptiness (loneliness) by surrendering our individuality and connecting our identity with the group in which we feel most compatible, those who affirm our beliefs, those from whom we draw the most comfort and support. We sacrifice our freedom when we escape to a situation in which no questions can be asked and answers are imposed authoritatively. In order to avoid the risk that we might be wrong, we passively surrender the right to ask and to doubt. (In fact Tillich believes that doubt is an essential condition of all spiritual life.)

Spiritual doubt often prompts a sense of guilt in the minds of some faithful Christians. I recall the night a football coach came to counsel with my father who was president of a college where the coach was employed. The man was fraught with guilt over his attempts to counteract his religious doubts and questions. He feared that it proved he was a weak and unfaithful Christian. My father listened carefully, and then consoled him: "No, Art. Even the disciples had doubts. It means you take your faith seriously." Belief searches for certainty. Faith lives in hope. After prayer and more conversation, the coach left our home comforted. "There is more faith in honest doubt, believe me, than in half the creeds," wrote Alfred Lord Tennyson.

While I find it difficult to absorb the depth and vastness of Tillich's writings, it seems that his theology and moral code were compartmentalized. His theology did not appear to inform moral decision making. Guilt was seemingly absent.

Fifty years ago, sitting in an ethics class lecture by the renowned ethicist, Dr. James Gustafson of Yale University, I listened as the professor departed from his notes and related an incident in which a friend had gone to Paul Tillich for marriage advice. The man confided to Tillich that, although he had been married to his wife for many years, he had recently fallen in love with a younger woman. He wondered if Tillich could help him resolve this internal struggle. Tillich advised the man to heed the passion in his heart and follow where it led. In other words, he was advising the man to ignore the moral strictures of his conscience and respect the impulses of his impassioned yearning.

Dr. Gustafson told us that he was stunned that Tillich would give such advice and give no consideration to the suffering which might ensue for the man's wife and family. Now, as I reflect on my reading of Hannah Tillich's revealing autobiography, that incident takes on new meaning. His theology did not necessarily inform his moral life. Should a person wrestle with the passions of his libido as vigorously as he does with the questions of his spiritual life? It is at this point that his theology might seem to reach a level of self-absorption, failing to consider the emotional involvement of partners or the sacrifice required by commitments.

The validity of the message, however, isn't necessarily dependent upon the character of the messenger. People with flawed character are capable of delivering inspired pronouncements. There are others who appear to be morally upright, yet are capable of evil. Hitler opposed abortion and pornography. He condemned all the things conservative Christians complained were ruining Germany. He denounced prostitution and drunkenness. He rebuked non-Christian religions. He glorified the image of piety even as he was carrying out the worst case of genocide in history.

Paul Tillich was raised in Germany, the son of a Lutheran minister. He became ordained in the Lutheran church and taught at universities in Germany. His early criticisms of Hitler led to his expulsion in 1933, along with many Jewish professors. He once observed that he became the first non-Jewish academician to be so honored. After immigrating to the United States, he became a citizen and taught for 32 years at New York's Union Theological Seminary, Harvard, and the University of Chicago.

## Seeking Truth

Many of us are too busy to spend time thinking about the significance of faith, human cruelty, eternity, or the existence of a supreme being. We become consumed with the details of daily life. We are caught up in the daily grind of responsibilities and escape the existential questions: *why am I here...what is my purpose?*

There comes a time in each person's life, however, when the stark realization of impermanence becomes unavoidable: the diagnosis of incurable cancer, the death of a child, the betrayal or abandonment of a husband or wife. It leads to hopeless despair.

This is when we may become receptive to the Judeo-Christian revelation that although we are dust and ashes, though we are nothing, yet we are something through a God who created and accepts us. Though we are unacceptable, we are accepted. Even a skeptic will consider that.

Reading these philosophies is enlightening. We are enriched by the diversity of views, reflecting on others' opinions and philosophical perceptions of reality. The perspectives of each religion or ethnic group offer us an enlarged view of the world in which we live: Buddhism, Muslim, Jew, Agnostic, Evangelical Christian.

I am not so arrogant as to claim that my beliefs are based on empirical evidence. In fact, I repeat, my creed is to renounce certitude (certainty) which is the cause of most human conflict. We must be willing to step back and listen to beliefs and points of view which are different from our own.

William James offers an alternative religious view in *The Will to Believe*, as does Alain de Botton in his book *Religion for Atheists: A Non-Believer's Guide to the Uses of Religion*. Botton even advances the pragmatic view that religion is "sporadically useful, interesting, and consoling" and can, therefore, be enlisted in the service of atheists."

Academic inquiry does not suppress the human spiritual instinct. At a time when atheism was fashionable among French intellectuals, Rene' Girard was an unabashed spokesman for what he called the "truths of Christianity." His prodigious work at John Hopkins and Stanford University covered the areas of anthropology, literature, psychology, and religion. He stood out among his French peers of atheists. He drew strength from his Catholic faith. He saw Christianity as one of the only potential sources for ending the history of human violence.

Religions — not religion in the abstract, but institutional religions — are "repositories" of good that can assuage human ills. I have witnessed the benefits of religious practices — prayers, rituals, feasts, music — to lift people's spirits, to alleviate despair, to heal broken relationships. In communities where politics incites division and disorder, spiritual compassion offers a nonviolent path to lasting peace.

## Notes

1 — The scriptural commandment second highest in prominence is "You shall not misuse the name of the Lord your God, for the Lord will not hold anyone guiltless who misuses his name." (NIV) There is no such biblical prohibition against using words referring to human sexual functions. Oddly though, many, especially those who claim a religious identity, are more offended by references to human sexuality (such as the "f--- word") than by "OMG" or "goddamned", which are scripturally prohibited by the second commandment. Why is that? Do we hold in higher reverence our human sexuality than the commandment that condemns cursing? Refined conversation avoids both.

The Germanic word (often mistakenly referred to as Anglo-Saxon or Old English) originally meant "to strike" or "to move back and forth." A legend claimed that once upon a time the population of England was decimated by a plague. So the king ordered his people to reproduce. His proclamation "Fornicate under command of the King" was supposedly the source of "F.U.C.K." This story is entertaining but untrue. The word may have first appeared only in the sixteenth century in the margin of an ancient manuscript by Latin orator Cicero, entitled *De Officiis* (A Guide to Moral Conduct). A monk who was reading this manuscript scrawled in the margin the words "O d fuckin Abbot." Beside it he wrote the date — 1528. He was probably expressing his disgust with a fellow monk who was having too much sex for someone sworn to celibacy. Interestingly, in his day the word "damned" was the real obscenity and could only be hinted at with the letter "d," similar to the way in which we often today write "f---" in publications.

2 — Greenblatt, Stephen. *The Swerve: How the World Became Modern.* W.W. Norton & Company, New York, 2011, page 144. Stephen Greenblatt is a literary historian and Professor of the Humanities at Harvard University. He writes about this corrupt period in church history with fascinating detail.

3 — Tillich, Hannah. *From Time to Time.* (New York, Stein and Day, 1973).

4 — Tillich, Paul. *The Courage to Be*, (New Haven, Connecticut Yale University Press, 2014).

# Chapter 12

# Doing The Right Thing, When The Right Thing Is Hard To Do

*There are many religions, but there is only one morality.*
John Ruskin

A management seminar speaker opened his remarks by asking the attendees, "Would you be happy working for someone like you? Why or why not?" Thinking about that question after I returned home from that seminar, made me skeptical about how I was running the company. I probably would not be happy working for someone like myself. I was too focused on the bottom line. I pushed my employees to work harder by measuring and monitoring and inspecting their activity. It often left me feeling frazzled and worried, and employees sensing that they were under constant surveillance. They were.

Weeks went by while I continued to fret about how I was running this multi-million dollar company. We were highly profitable, but nobody was having any fun, especially me. I was up late every night dreaming new marketing plans, drafting cost reduction strategies, setting new sales goals.

Now I had to consider the piece of the puzzle I had neglected: "Would you be happy working for you?" Since my answer was "probably not," I spent the next few weeks reframing my business approach.

I worked with my financial officer and accountant to establish a profit sharing plan. But since that reward was only granted once a year, I searched for ways to provide more immediate methods of positive reinforcement by recognizing extra effort. I started to give small cash bonuses for outstanding performance. I learned that praise can be as effective and motivating as monetary gifts. I looked for any excuse to recognize achievement, instead of mistakes. I learned that when correction is necessary, it should be noted verbally in private. Positive performance, on the other hand, should be recognized in writing and given wider recognition.

I repressed my pessimistic nature by greeting every employee with a big smile in the morning, even a joke to show that I *did* have a sense of humor after all. (This simple inspiration came to me after reading that Jack Welch's successful management style at General Electric was what he called, "Managing by walking around." He knew the name of every GE employee and used it in greeting as many as possible throughout the company.)

At the end of three months I became aware that employees were more forthright with me, suggesting changes that would increase sales and reduce costs. Several months later I met with a few key leaders to plan an employee recognition day. They came up with the idea of closing the company for a day (what? how much would that cost?) and taking everyone to Cedar Point Amusement Park for a day of fun and celebration. The event was featured on the front page of the local paper, with a picture of the company and all the smiling employees. Free advertising and company recognition! And I received a large batch of employee applications over the next few weeks.

Ethical teaching is not exclusive to religion. People who go to church every Sunday may not necessarily conduct themselves according to a higher moral standard than those who never listen to a sermon, read a Bible, or sing a hymn. Moral behavior is often guided by pragmatism. What can I get away with and not get caught? How do you act when no one is looking? Would you act differently if you could become invisible? This applies to a moral decision as simple as giving back incorrect change from a clerk, or willfully neglecting to report all your income on a tax return.

An insurance company conducted an experiment to determine how trustworthy employees would be when they were asked to pay voluntarily for items provided in a coffee break room. A sign on the wall above a coffee pot requested a fifty-cent payment for each cup of coffee. At the end of the test period it was evident that only a few of the coffee drinkers had deposited the payment. Subsequently, an 8" x 10" picture was hung on the wall behind the coffee pot. It showed a stern-faced man whose eyes appeared to be staring directly at each person who approached the coffee pot. Even though it was only a picture, 95% of the coffee drinkers paid up. How honest are we? How are ethical decisions made? You answer that.

Moral behavior is shaped by early childhood instruction. Our first instinct is self-preservation. Learning to do the right thing, when the right thing is hard to do, comes later, influenced by adult example and instruction. The inflection points of history are often marked by strong leaders who are willing to defy consensus, sometimes to the point of self-sacrifice in order to "do the right thing." It was such bravery that led to the elimination of slavery in a new nation whose economy had been built on that institution. It required the courage of brave individuals to defy Hitler and defeat Nazism. Doing the right thing may require self-deprivation or sacrifice to achieve a greater good.

A degree of other-directedness is necessary for anyone who hopes to be a contributing member of a family or community. We use the term sociopath to describe people who are incapable of concern for others, and who care only about their own needs and desires.

Does religious affiliation raise our moral sensitivity or make us more law abiding? Does religious teaching make us more generous? Biblical passages encourage unselfishness. There are almost thirty references to "conscience" in the New Testament. The letters of Saint Paul instruct followers to keep a clear conscience not only before God, but also to be aware of obligations to others. At times these obligations may supersede what might be in one's own best interest. This is when 'doing the right thing' may be hard to do.

"Among your brothers in any of the towns of the land that the Lord your God is giving you, do not be hardhearted or tightfisted toward your poor brother. Rather be openhanded and freely lend him whatever he needs" (Deuteronomy 15:7-8). Numerous New Testament passages promote benevolence: "It is more blessed to give than to receive (Acts 20:35). 1 Timothy 6:17-19 admonishes those who have more than they need, "to be generous and ready to share." 2 Corinthians 9:6 warns against stingy behavior, and promises that those who give bountifully will also reap bountifully. Throughout the Bible, generosity is one of the cardinal rules of spiritual life.

However, factors other than spirituality often guide our altruism. Statistics show that those who are most willing to share earn less than $25,000 a year. Living close to the poverty line raises sensitivity to the pain of deprivation. The percentage of giving drops as earnings rise to $75,000 a year. Those who earn above $200,000 per year, give a lower percentage of their income to charitable causes on average. Those who have less seem more willing to share. Those who have more become attached to their wealth. They become fearful of losing it, and derive a sense of security from holding on to more of it.

Religious teaching overlays a higher level of authority onto ethical behavior by asserting the spiritual connection to human activity. The Judeo-Christian religion promotes an ethical ideal that does not come naturally to human instinct. *Love your enemy. Do good to those who curse you. Observe a day of rest and worship. Refrain from desiring your neighbor's property or possessions.*

The most important ethical requirement according to the Bible is to love God and love your neighbor as yourself. How might a practical application of these commandments play out in an American household? Maybe the family dinner table discussion would go something like this:

"The lady in the grocery store was wearing a head covering. She must be a Muslim. Let's see what we can find out about Islam and talk about it tomorrow at dinner."

"That girl who lives by herself with three little kids was screaming at them when we drove by. She must be under a lot of pressure. Let's discuss what we can do to help her."

"A black family was looking at the house across the street that's for sale. How can we show that we are culturally advanced neighbors without seeming to be patronizing?"

## Spiritual Life And Human Emotion

I understand the power of anger that can burn against every nerve and consume my attention. During my three score and plus years I remember those bitter moments when my brain was on fire. I wish I could forget those emotions; I wish that they would evaporate the way my nocturnal dreams disappear as soon as I awaken. When they lasted like a simmering brew of poison, I had to find a way to diminish their power.

*She ridiculed me and when she saw how angry I was, she laughed in my face.*

*I thought he was a friend upon whom I could rely; then he betrayed me.*

*He promised to pay me back. Now I realize he had no intention to do so.*

*I thought I knew him; I never realized what a bigot he was.*

*She lied about me and made fun of me behind my back.*

How do we resolve the hostility, the anger that simmers over a rejection, an undeserved insult? This bitterness brews and destroys peace of mind.

I go into a museum or a cathedral where the majesty of art and architecture surround me. What could have inspired anyone to create such massive grandeur? Its source could only have been drawn from a higher dimension. It opens a world that is larger than my anger; a human capacity for creativity that is far above the source of my fury and depression.

Hostility can destroy my peace of mind, while doing nothing to diminish my foe. I discover that the only way to cure obsessive anger is to reframe the circumstances. I acknowledge the repulsion, which is damaging only to me. I picture the betrayer as a conflicted, suffering human being who has been emotionally damaged. I start by finding a small space for pity, sympathy — even sorrow — for his humanity; for her insecurity. In a sense, it becomes a transition through the pathos of prayer. Is this employing spiritual practice for personal healing? Is it self-serving? Or is it reaching for a lifeline to survival? It's not an original idea. It wasn't mine to begin with. *Bless those who curse you, pray for those who mistreat you* (Luke 6:28). This is 2000-year-old psychotherapy; a miracle of emotional healing.

# Chapter 13

# Restoring Intellectual Challenge

*There lies more faith in honest doubt, believe me,*
*than in half the creeds.*
    Alfred Lord Tennyson

A restless night of bad dreams and anxiety was followed by morning hours that did nothing to improve my spirits. By mid-morning I was ready for the day to end. My canine companion had other ideas. She looked at me from her bed. When I met her gaze she jumped up, walked over to me and licked my hand, then ran to where she had hidden one of her tennis balls. She returned and dropped it in my lap. It was the signal for the mid-morning routine: the fifteen minutes of running to retrieve the ball, activity that brings her pure ecstasy. This is higher on her list than chewing on a steak bone. Oh that my human spirit could be elevated by such simple pleasures.

After several retrievals, she lies down on the ground in front of me, her heart pounding. I lie down beside her, wondering if grass would stain my shirt or a cinch bug would crawl up my pant leg. I hear her sigh. I take a deep breath. I feel the earth absorb my stress, anxiety being absorbed into the ground. This is nothing like the nap in bed to recover from fatigue. How long had it been since I had felt this close to the earth; nature, the primordial mother? I neglect her nurturing at my own risk. The infinite sky reminds me of how small I am: a spec of an organism, existing for a brief moment on the continuum of a billion years. By the third generation my name will be forgotten. This humble reminder of my connection to nature serves me well.

We run barefoot in the grass until we are five. We roll on the ground, play in the dirt. As we get older we move farther and farther away from the earth. We lose our connection. The Japanese have endorsed a way to restore it. They call it forest bathing. It became a national public health program in 1982. Nothing is prescribed except to relax, sit, or meander among the trees; it requires no counting of steps, no measuring of distance. Studies have shown that it lowers the heart rate, and the blood pressure. It elevates the immune system and reduces stress hormones.

*Therefore do not worry about tomorrow, for tomorrow will worry about itself. Each day has enough troubles of its own (Matthew 6:34).*

"In the street and in society I am almost invariably cheap and dissipated, my life is unspeakably mean," Thoreau wrote in his diary in 1857. "No amount of gold or respectability would in the least redeem it — dining with the Governor or a member of Congress. But alone in distant woods or fields, in unpretending sprout lands or pastures tracked by rabbits, even on a black, and, to most, cheerless day like this…I come to myself, I once more feel myself grandly related, and that the cold and solitude are friends of mine. I suppose that this value, in my case, is equivalent to what others get by churchgoing and prayer."[1]

I have expended considerable energy during my seventy plus years trying to avoid admitting ignorance. There have been times when I have bungled my way through a business meeting in Italy, laughing as though I understood the joke when a fellow executive at the conference table, speaking in Italian, pointed at me and laughed, or when an acronym that represented an obscure corporate policy or financial formula was used. I faked my way through it just so I wouldn't have to say, 'What does that mean?' It's a blow to the ego when someone says, "You mean you were formerly a minister and you don't know what Balaam's donkey spoke to him?" (Number 22:27f) Ignorance is weakness, right? I should have remembered my fourth-grade teacher's admonition, "There's no such thing as a stupid question." But I listened to the cautious voice of my ego, 'Better to remain silent and be thought a fool, than to open your mouth and remove all doubt.'

Even more difficult than 'I don't know' is the admission "I was wrong." Someone said it this way: The three hardest things to do in life are not physical feats or intellectual achievements, but moral acts: to include the excluded, to return love for hate, and to say *I was wrong.* I can't remember the last time I said that, even though I remember being wrong as recently as this morning. The strange part is that whenever I have heard someone else make that confession, I have admired the person more, not less, for admitting it.

I am emotionally attached to most of my beliefs. And I have encountered that uncomfortable moment when a belief I held with certitude turned out to be untrue. It was like gradually coming to the realization that there is no Santa Claus. Stubborn certitude has been around as long as people could shout their opinions:

*Of course the world is flat!*

*It's humanly impossible for a runner to break the four minute mile!*

*I don't care what the majority of earth scientists say. Global warming is simply the result of cyclical climate trends.*[2]

That's when Snoopy whispers, "Did it ever occur to you that you might be wrong?"

The most reliable research confirms the existence of climate change that is driven by human activity. The United States and other countries have poured billions of tons of carbon dioxide and methane into the atmosphere, resulting in increased frequency of extreme heat events. The evidence is measured by towers, buoys, and satellites and analyzed by thousands of scientists around the world. The most serious skeptics are now agreeing with the indisputable evidence, according to the president of the Environmental Defense Fund.

A few continue to claim that temperature change is due to normal cycles in the earth's atmosphere. However, in the fullness of time, earth scientists tell us that the laws of nature dictate that our sun, which is but one of a billion stars in the galaxy, will eventually expand, boil away the oceans, and incinerate the planet. What then? Apparently human life will become as extinct as the dinosaurs. No life as we know it could exist.

Humanity may be lucky to survive its own self-destructive impulses. Nations around the world build their military capabilities, creating nuclear bombs that could destroy most of the human race if they all entered into another world war. The United States will spend over $886 billion in the next year on military defense. That is four times the size of China's military budget, which is under $200 billion. Russia spends less than $60 billion. The US spends more on its military budget than the next eight nations combined. This begs the question of how much destructive capability a country needs to defend itself. How many tanks, troops, bombs, how many countries at one time must the US be prepared to attack with over three-quarters of a trillion dollars?

Unilateralists like John Bolton claim that treaties with allies are too weak, and that dictators defy the limits of treaties anyway. Rather than seeking multilateral agreements and cooperative efforts we must develop our own super-weapons. Unfortunately today even third-rate countries are doing the same. Countries from Japan and North Korea to Saudi Arabia, Turkey and Egypt are developing weapons of mass destruction. Nuclear programs continue to proliferate around the world even as scientists conclude that they cannot be used without threatening the end of human civilization.

A risk that is even more imminent than a nuclear holocaust is the selective devastation that a targeted cyberattack can produce. In 2017, North Korea and Russia engaged in cyberattacks that crippled the British health care system and devastated Ukraine, disrupted shipping and shut down factories. The Washington administration called it a billion-dollar attack that was "the most destructive and costly in history."[3] The attack came without warning to any intelligence agency.

Department of Homeland Securities acknowledged that in 2017 Russian hackers infiltrated dozens of US electrical utilities. An attack on our banking system, our hospitals, even our cars and security cameras, which are all internet connected, could leave us utterly defenseless. Gas pumps could become inoperative, life support in hospitals would be unavailable, and transportation would be shut down. And because these are under no central government control, no authority in our country would be prepared to issue a counter-attack, or present a plan to implement it.

While the media has focused primarily on the interference with our political elections, less attention has been drawn to how Russian experts have been able to gain access to our grid systems. They have the ability to disable the traffic signals in major cities, the airline and train information systems on line, disrupting travel across the country and around the world. Such attacks would render impotent our $800 billion investment in soldiers, tanks, and bombers, because no commands could be issued or received and no communication system would be available to coordinate their activity.

Could the United States choose to deploy military expenditures more strategically: for example to bribe carefully chosen insiders to assassinate a malicious dictator? The answer to that question is a closely guarded secret by the Central Intelligence Agency. Considerations of this kind run up against ethical judgments of international diplomacy. We know that in 1973 the CIA was involved in an attempt to take down the Allende government in Chile. Congress has made attempts to intervene in clandestine CIA operations. In 1975 the Senate select committee under the direction of Senator Frank Church investigated the CIA's attempt to kill Fidel Castro. Intelligence work requires the agency to act as judge and jury, at times suppressing moral sensitivities.

Consider, however, that instead of spending $610 million on a single B-21 jet bomber, a group of dissident foreign insiders in just three countries ruled by vile leaders could be contracted for $200 million each to capture or assassinate those corrupt dictators who have committed crimes against humanity. Their assassination would be equivalent to capital punishment. Brutal dictators who defy international law prohibiting the use of poison gas, who threaten with nuclear arsenals, who starve, burn, and incarcerate their own people, could be eliminated at a fraction of the cost that would result from a war of nuclear bombing or devastating ground war with soldiers, tanks, and bombs, which result in the deaths of thousands of innocent civilians. The execution of malicious rulers would save millions of lives.

Meanwhile, our military spending could be reduced and used to build a more efficient system of transportation, a more secure cyber security system, improved health care (where we rate twenty-third in the world), and an infrastructure plan for the future.

This was the direction that President Dwight Eisenhower pointed to when he stated in a speech to the American Society of Newspaper Editors in 1953: *Every gun that is made, every warship launched, every rocket fired signifies, in the final sense, a theft from those who hunger and are not fed, those who are cold and not clothed...The cost of one modern heavy bomber is this: a modern brick school in more than 30 cities. It is two electric power plants, each serving a town with a population of 60,000. It is two fine, fully equipped hospitals. It is some 50 miles of concrete pavement.*

Convictions can create blinders to reality. A conviction can defy all the evidence...because we refuse to believe that it's evidence. This means we never have to say, "I was wrong." We dislike those who remind us of our errancy. When we analyze achievement we discover that most successful people are able to consider the possibility that they are wrong, to embrace uncertainty.

The older we get the more we crave the comfort of certainty. Skepticism, self-doubt, feels like weakness, failure even. Age ossifies our bones and our spirits. We are less flexible — both physically and emotionally. We seek permanence. We want to stay in one place. Stress stimulates the need for stability. We become religiously dogmatic. We avoid any political opinions that differ from our beliefs. We seek and find comfort in those who agree with our views.

"Only two more weeks before we can get rid of that idiot in the White House," someone fumed on Facebook a while back. I had to bite my tongue to keep from responding to such a meaningless, spiteful statement. The shallow expression contained nothing informative. It didn't attempt to offer any reasoning or basis for discussion. It simply vented the hostility of an individual who was ill disposed to anyone who didn't think, speak, or look like her. Oh well. We who can't resist sharing our screed have to admit that Facebook is little more than an exhibitionist compulsion; a viral plague of social media. Some have called it the highest level of narcissism.

But just to make clear who that rant referred to, it was posted on Facebook in January 2009. George Bush was the president. A conservative news article admitted that he was one of the most disliked presidents in recent history. I voted for George Bush. But on each successive trip to Italy to attend board meetings over the previous eight years, I had noticed the growing hostility toward our president, the hate messages that were appearing in the newspaper headlines and the graffiti on the train walls: "Death to Americans," and "Kill George Bush."

*The world is a book and those who don't travel read only a page.*
Augustine

Today there is similar international opposition growing against President Trump. At the start of his presidency many of his advisors asked him to desist from sending out his syntactically simple midnight tweets. Now the public has become accustomed to them and his Republican critics have abandoned their attempts to restrain him. The tweets are a distraction from topics that threaten his credibility, and he continues to speak to his core supporters.

He has criticized President Obama as being a failed president, intentionally disguising the fact that the US stock market delivered better returns under Obama than almost any previous president. The tax cuts and the Recovery Act in 2009 gave credence to the claim Obama made that, "It's a phenomenal time to be an investor." Those who followed his advice more than tripled their money even before dividends. But biases and political polarities blind party loyalists to experience and reality.

✠ ✠ ✠

My objective is to avoid rigid certitude, to accept the value of each person and respect his/her opinion. I strive to refrain from dismissing others on the basis of their political or religious beliefs, while at the same time reserving the right to question how they arrived at their assumptions. I don't expect all my associates to interpret religious and political issues as I do. And no matter how difficult it is to listen, I will attempt to respect our mutual right to hold opposing views. My goal is to improve not only my own understanding of a controversial issue, but my insight into the fascinating differences in human nature.

Robert, an executive with an international manufacturing company, is firm in his support of President Trump. Because of our mutual respect for each other, we have been able to discuss our contrary views respectfully. At my request Robert reviewed chapters 7 and 13 of this book. He responded with helpful suggestions and statements that justify his support of President Trump. I have edited parts of my writing based on his suggestions.

Robert: "If Trump had a title, it might be *The Great Disruptor.* I think many Americans are looking for some disruption in the pay-to-play politics, and the stagnation that describes our government. Many of us want a bold president; not that we agree with everything he does or says, but we are willing to give him a pass to see where it leads."

I have informed Robert that I listen to news commentators from both the left and the right, not only to avoid unjustified bias, but also to gain a broader picture of the American public. Like others, I am more readily drawn to information that confirms my political assumptions. It means I won't have to deal with contrary evidence. Psychologists call this *confirmation bias.* It is human nature, but it's a self-limiting proposition. Ben Tappin and Ryan McKay at the University of London have conducted experiments that reveal how desperately we *want* to hang on to our political beliefs, despite new evidence that proves them wrong. No one wants to be shown he is wrong, and, except in the case of the most intellectually objective minds, new evidence is generally received with emotional resistance before it is even thought out. We avoid evidence that challenges our beliefs. We may all be somewhat like Donald Trump, who said to one biographer, "I don't like to analyze myself because I might not like what I see." Psychiatrists diagnose this as pathological self-reduction, such as the characteristic of sacrificing the right to self-reflection, even about one's own point of view.

Effective leaders understand the need for self-evaluation, the ability to look calmly at both sides of difficult issues. They become skilled at negotiating agreement. Certitude doesn't lead to growth or consensus building. It is divisive. In business or politics it is a losing characteristic.

It is helpful for me to engage in an unemotional exchange of ideas with a person like Robert: "Trump did not create the immigration issues — those laws were already on the books and Congress has failed to take care of the root problem." A recent Wall Street Journal/NBC News Poll, however, indicates that 51% disapprove of Mr. Trump's handling of border security. An even higher percentage — 58% — disapproves of his treatment of parents and children who have been separated after entering the country illegally.

Insecurity makes us intolerant of people who don't agree with us. Politics and religion can be divisive subjects even among close family members. Political rancor has become more prominent in our day than at any other period in our lifetime. It has caused irreversible ruptures in some of our friendships. In order to tolerate one another, we carefully avoid the issues in which there is no possibility for calm discussion of policy differences.

Robert: "Trump is winning back the independent voters and any of the Republican voters whom he may have lost in the first six months. I watch CNN every morning and am amazed that they continue to spend more than 90% of their news on Trump (all of it negative) even though they continue to lose viewers."

News commentators on both sides drive us farther apart with their ramped up rhetoric and twisting of truths. A man being interviewed by a Fox commentator noted that Trump had run on a campaign of building a wall *that Mexico would pay for*. The Fox commentator responded, "He (Trump) never said that!" How can we carry on meaningful discussions when the media manufacture history to say whatever they want it to be?

A small percentage of individuals get their national news information exclusively from the Fox News television channel. When I checked into my hotel room in Chicago, the cleaning lady was just finishing her tasks. She had the television turned to a Sean Hannity news program. "Do you also watch other news stations," I asked her?

"No, I keep the TV tuned to Fox all day."

"How do you know what other people might be thinking and watching," I asked?

"I don't care what anybody else thinks," she told me as she pushed her cleaning cart out of the room.

Seeking truth becomes a difficult challenge when we are faced with unreliable information that is often a careful selection of facts chosen to support a well-defined agenda. Few are intellectually curious and skeptical enough to conduct their own research. Most are unwilling to consider opinions that challenge their own. They assume an unquestioning infallibility and become irritated at any attempt to examine their suppositions.

Changing our way of thinking, or our way of life, may only occur as a result of a serious mishap; maybe a near crisis. Consider the amusing story of the man who saw a beautiful blonde light up a large cigar as she sat on a bench at the playground where her child was playing. The man was so surprised that he asked, how did you ever begin smoking cigars? She said, "Oh, it was really quite simple. One evening my husband came home and found a lighted cigar in our living room ashtray."

Drastic circumstances may require drastic change. In some cases words or explanations will not resolve the issue. It may simply be too difficult to talk about it. Silence is the best mediator at times. Nothing can be gained from rancorous accusations.

Our rhetoric becomes less effective when we attempt to overpower someone with our opinion. The skill of effective argumentation teaches that we should ask questions, and seek common ground. The power of persuasion can become buried under ridicule and scorn.

Steven Levitsky and Daniel Ziblatt have written in *How Democracies Die*:[4] "If one thing is clear from studying breakdowns throughout history, it's that extreme polarization can kill democracies." How close are we to that extreme today?

*Nick*, a friend and President of an S&P 500 company wrote to me: "I didn't vote for the President, but it is of some surprise to me that the traditional shapers of American opinion do not look more deeply into the roots of his win. Nick demonstrates a perceptive insight into the mind of those working people who voted for Trump; an unbiased reflection that is missing from most political discussion.

*Nick:* "The Trump victory was almost completely unexpected with most interested parties predicting a Clinton landslide right up to Election Day. It might be asserted that even casual curiosity would lead to a perspective beyond the relatively simple and commonly-voiced explanations that are spread across the electorate. Even to this day, the general response to the Trump election appears to be inhabited with at least some significant share of anger, embarrassment, and dismissal...not solid bases for accurate understanding or analysis.

"I believe if our leaders in Washington, New York or in the major universities looked more closely, they would see that President Trump is in office because he represented himself as prioritizing the interests of everyday people...an orientation mostly unalloyed by other considerations. Indeed, since election, the President has exhibited a primary focus on the concerns of the people who placed him in office. In his inauguration address, he said 'Every decision on trade, on taxes, on immigration, on foreign affairs, on international strategy, will be made to benefit American workers and American families.' To those who are puzzled by the President's program, I offer that it's somewhat more coherent if viewed through the lens of...not American business or American economics...but of, simply, American jobs. This is the orientation that authored his election and, from a macro perspective, he appears to be following that direction."

Nick's balanced analysis reflects the wisdom of our early founding fathers: "We must try to find a way to see citizens on the other side as cousins who are...never our mortal enemies" (John Adams).

✠ ✠ ✠

A toxic political environment raises discussion to emotional levels where reason is replaced with rant. It forces us to take sides. The middle ground where problems are normally resolved no longer exists.

There are two schools of thought with regard to the efficacy of Donald Trump's political style. Those who view him favorably describe him as a pugilistic New York street fighter who will ultimately cause his foes (he includes in this category any country with whom the US has a trade deficit) to cry uncle and bow to their knees. He will no longer allow the US to sacrifice economic interests in order to be the diplomatic leader of the free world, or provide foreign military protection so that countries may have more resources for their own economic interests. His crude rhetoric, they claim, is nothing to be concerned about, because it is simply his fighting style. Criticism of his language is simplistic and avoids the more important discussion of policy objectives. Defenders of his crass vocabulary search for comparable remarks of former politicians to justify his simple communication style. And they are not difficult to dig up. Republicans were quick to denounce Vice President Joe Biden who whispered into Obama's ear, "This is a big fucking deal!" Fox News was the first to broadcast it and repeatedly ran it on air in order to humiliate Biden. John Garner, vice president under FDR, made the famous declaration that "the vice-presidency isn't worth a pitcher of warm piss." We remember when camera's caught George Bush declaring that a *The New York Times* journalist was a "major-league asshole." Trump gets a pass from his supporters on his choice of raw vocabulary.

On the other side, there are those who argue that Trump's off-the-cuff remarks and late night tweets indicate a naïve attitude toward the complex art of diplomacy; he has no defined policy objective, they say, and his defiant approach is dangerous. He called the European Union a top foe of our country while embracing Russia's Vladimir Putin as a great leader. He claims that after withdrawing the US from the Trans-Pacific Partnership and the Iran nuclear agreement, as well as threatening to pull out of the North American Free Trade Agreement, he will replace all these with "something better." His tariff war, which he claims is "easy to win," is threatening small businesses. His methods may have worked in the business arena, but the theater of world politics is more complicated and requires skillful diplomacy and the cultivation of allies. His advisors have indicated that he operates by instinct and shows little interest in preparing for meetings with world leaders. He may prove to be a more successful disruptor than arbitrator. Speaker of the House Paul Ryan claims that he has repeatedly prevented tragedies which might have occurred if he, Ryan, had not restrained Trump.

Robert: "Trump opponents may be underestimating his strategy. A trade war could result in two positive results: first it can provide some restraint to an overheating economy which can lead to increased interest rates; second, it may very well help reduce some of the unfair trade balance that exists, especially in the case of China. Trump's negotiating style may appear to be brash or extreme. But the history of his business practice has been to ask for far more than he expects to get, in order to move the needle back to the middle. And getting some kind of deal with North Korea, China, and the EU trade rebalancing, keeping the economy going and some movement with immigration reform can only help him."

The moral character of a president is still valued by most Americans, but virtuous behavior does not necessarily equate with wisdom in governance. High-minded piety may inspire compassion and moral rectitude, but it does not guarantee an aptitude for making tough policy decisions.

Exceptional knowledge of American history, however, is a necessity for wise leadership in the White House. When the president claims that a football player who kneels for the national anthem should be "kicked out of the country," he reveals his ignorance of the Supreme Court ruling over seven decades ago that ruled it unconstitutional to coerce recognition or observance of national symbols. And he displays a shallow understanding of military complexity when he declares that his solution to defeating ISIS is to "bomb the shit out of them. I would just bomb those suckers." These character traits make it difficult to evaluate objectively the efficacy of his strategic goals. (Some insiders claim he has none.) His outsized personality, unfortunately, overshadows dispassionate analysis of his economic and diplomatic objectives.

Skepticism is not part of Donald Trump's character. His stump speeches reveal a bold self-confidence. He has a sixth sense for how he can appeal to his base. "I love the poorly educated," he has claimed repeatedly. "I'm really rich, Trump likes to say. Or the long form: "Part of the beauty of me is that I am very rich."[5]

Supporters of the Trump presidential style are quick to excuse him in order to avoid admitting the possible error of their support. It's easier to defend signs of the president's weakness than to accept the disturbing challenge to their own opinions. Psychologists describe this emotion as cognitive dissonance. When two parts of reality are in conflict, it causes annoyance. You need to eliminate one of them. Like the feeling the smoker gets when an anti-smoking ad appears on television. Changing the channel is easier than dealing with the discomfort of acknowledging a bad habit. In politics, it's easier to ignore the evidence of Trump's duplicity than to admit an error of judgment. Most Trump supporters keep the television tuned to Fox.

Our political judgments are grounded in emotional bias. We apply a different standard to the political leaders we favor. We approve or disapprove depending on who made the claim. Kick an athlete out of the country for bowing instead of saluting? Bomb the shit out of a foreign adversary? I'm a brave solider for surviving intercourse with multiple women without incurring VD? Those words from the lips of a black man would have buried any chances of political success. And getting elected president of the United States after making such claims would have been impossible. Hence the old admonishment to young black children from their parents: 'you have to be twice as good.'

The judgments we make about a political figure are not based on an objective analysis, but are determined by emotional bias. We respond either with dismissive excuses or repulsion, depending upon our personal unreflective bias. The greatest challenge we face is to keep the dialogue open between citizens on both sides. Once our differences prevent us from talking to each other, our democracy is diminished.

Both defenders and detractors say that the president could help us raise the level of political civility if he would speak in the manner of our country's previous presidents, whose discourse reflected mutual respect. Thomas Jefferson wrote to John Adams: *That you and I differ in our idea of the best form of government is well known to us both, but we have differed as friends should do, respecting the purity of each other's motives, and confiding our differences of opinion to private conversation.*

I would welcome the solemnity of this style of discourse among our political leaders. It would help to reduce the wide gulf that now separates the left from the right, and it would redirect our attention from personality to policy-making.

Robert: "Nothing you have written upsets me in the least, but you had already informed me of your own bias, and had welcomed my rebuttal. While I do remain a Trump supporter, like most, I do not support everything he does or says, but what I support in his administration is more important than what I reject. If I had to vote again today, knowing what I know about Trump, I would still vote for him." Most of us don't possess this degree of emotional control with respect to our political adversaries. I am grateful for this rare opportunity. It might lead to that middle ground where the best conclusions are reached.

I am convinced that constructive dialogue is the only way to arrive at common values. I have continued to reflect on the common sense approach that Nick, the president of a US corporation, has written to me in our dialog.

*Nick:* "There is much discussion regarding the President's style in pursuing his goals. As has been stated, it's not clear that his supporters agree with all of his actions or statements. Actually, I'm not sure this is necessarily a new phenomenon. Supporters of previous Presidents may have shared that reservation regarding some of those past leader's actions. Regarding our current President, however, I do believe there is quite a gulf between the views held by many in Washington, New York, and in other seats of intellectual leadership, such as universities, and the perspectives inhabiting the vehicle repair shops of places like Peoria, Illinois, and the factories of places like Algona, Iowa. Those who might characterize themselves as thought-leaders in our capitals often do not seem to take Donald Trump seriously as a President, but they do seem to take everything he says seriously. On the other hand, the people in the factories and in the shops, the people of everyday work, tend to take him seriously as a President, but they generally appear to take little of what he says seriously. I believe these alternate perspectives are a principal explanation for the differing reactions to the President that exist across the country."

It's been almost forty years since the national best-selling book *Getting to Yes: Negotiating Agreement without Giving In*[6] was published. The book was the result of Harvard's Program on Negotiation. It emphasizes the necessity of understanding the other person's point of view. "Ultimately… conflict lies not in objective reality, but in people's heads. Truth is simply one more argument — perhaps a good one, perhaps not — for dealing with the difference." The study shows that "getting to yes" requires careful listening, withholding judgment, and discussing each other's perceptions. The book should be a required text in every public school and college.

Several years ago I visited a business on the West coast which our company had bought. The two founders of the business had a falling out and treated each other with a vitriolic acrimony. Their rancor permeated the entire workplace. It was evident from the moment one entered the front door. Anything either one of them proposed was immediately rejected by the other. It had reached the point at which they avoided coming within fifty feet of each other. Whatever instruction was presented to employees by one of them would be immediately reversed by the other. My job was to seek a way to achieve compromise, some kind of middle ground that would allow them to begin speaking to each other.

Using a counseling method employed to divert married couples from heading to divorce, I asked for a meeting of the three of us. I explained the ground rules: each one was to be given five minutes to state his expectations of the company: the goals and the method to achieve them. He could also include what he saw as obstacles, but the session was not to be focused on criticism of the other partner. During that five minute period the other partner must sit and listen without comment. Each partner then would be given five minutes to explain what he had heard the other one say, without offering any judgment or rebuttal.

As soon as I was done explaining these ground rules, the older of the two partners stood up livid with rage. "That's ridiculous," he said, "I refuse to do that. In fact I will not sit here a moment longer."

Obviously, that left no room for healing or compromise. The malevolence had created a rupture that was beyond restoration. We terminated both partners and brought the business in house.

*"It takes a great man to be a good listener."*
Calvin Coolidge

Intercollegiate debate required the skill of quick thinking and analytical listening. College debate competition half a century ago was as exciting as college football competition is today. Our debate coach trained us in how to listen as well as what to listen for, in order to respond with sensible logic and well-constructed rebuttals. When entering a debate competition we were not told until the last minute whether we would be arguing for or against an issue. We had to be prepared to argue either side, pro or con. It didn't matter what our personal conviction was. The topic at our state tournament one year was capital punishment. My personal attitude favored it, but I had to be prepared to present a convincing argument in opposition to it. Reaching the level of state competition was the ultimate goal, and when we reached that level it felt like we had qualified for the Rose Bowl.

If these debate tournaments were conducted today, the university might be obligated to provide a "safe place" in which a student could recover when confronted with a challenging argument. Topics such as abortion, immigration, or gender equality, would trigger some tender sensibilities and undoubtedly not survive the condemnation of the PC police. Choice of words is carefully monitored in higher education and infractions can bring severe consequences.

Massachusetts' Mount Holyoke College, an all-female student school, issued a guide to professors advising them to refrain from using the word "women" when describing the school's female population. Banning that word will help "foster intersectionality in the classroom" (whatever that means) the administration claims.

Social media increases the opportunity to share political opinions; and when those opinions are offensive or contrary to our views, we can simply "unfriend" the person who posted them. Turning off disagreeable information relieves us of composing an intelligent rebuttal.

Pedagogical instruction today emphasizes the importance of emotional sensitivity of the instructor; the ability of a teacher to show compassion, to recognize "trigger warnings." These are important insights, for learning is not exclusively a rational process. However, emotional sensitivity must be balanced with instruction in the discipline (perhaps even the art?) of emotional control. Outside the classroom those whom we encounter will be oblivious to our emotional sensitivity. A boss, a co-worker, even a family member will not be likely to recognize or show deference to our emotional delicacy. Learning how to respond to uncomfortable information would improve our relationships at home, at work, and in our social lives.

Debate has been replaced with Facebook posts, which more often than not, have no factual basis. Water cooler discussions are debased with the use of slurs, epithets, and name-calling instead of factual evidence. It has become permissible to reject the views of others without providing a thoughtful argument. Rant and exaggeration have replaced civil discourse.

Formalized debate competition has all but disappeared from university curricula. One of its primary benefits was the obligation to be exposed to the opposition, and then to use logic, evidence, and facts to support or rebut an issue. John Stuart Mill said, "He who knows only his own side of the case, knows little of that."

When a conservative scholar representing the American Enterprise Institute arrived to give a talk at the Lewis and Clark Law School in Portland, Oregon, she was met with protestors who blocked the entrance. She was able to enter the building through a side entrance, but when she reached the podium, "several sign-wielding students dashed to the front of the room…with chants of 'black lives matter,' and 'micro-aggressions are real,' but they got their way." The speech was cut short.[7] We have come a long way from collegiate debate to law school students who are unable to tolerate uncomfortable information.

We are divided in our country today by our language, our religion, and our politics. We are becoming more alienated from members of our own family and from our next door neighbor. The next prophet will be a voice crying in the wilderness, calling for compassion and compromise — for character over charisma, for virtue over prestige and achievement over money.

But will we listen?

# Notes

1 — Thoreau, Henry David, *Selections from the Journals*, edited by Walter Harding, Dover Thrift Editions, 1995.

2 — William Vollmann's book *Carbon Ideologies* is mentioned by Ted Hamilton in **Boston Review**. Eric Allen Been in **Vox. com** writes that Vollman spent seven years "crunching data, circling the globe and interviewing coal miners and energy industry CEOs, eventually spending his own money to complete the project." He concluded that there was simply too much financial incentive to discontinue those practices that are destroying the environment. So much of what experts warn about is invisible, which makes it easy to ignore. Vollman thinks that it's already too late to avert disaster. "It's going to be a very, very ugly society," he says. "Hopefully, you and I will be safely dead before things get to be too bad." (*The Week* magazine June 1, 2018 edition.)

Scientists make a distinction between "global warming" which refers to the earth's rising surface temperature, and "climate change" which includes warming and the side effects of warming — melting glaciers, more frequent drought and flooding. Climate change can involve human causes as well as natural causes. Burning fossil fuels, using aerosol sprays, and deforestation all play a part in the reflection of sunlight and the carbon-storing capacity of forests.

While the earth's climate has experienced fluctuating temperatures throughout its four billion-year history because of changes in its orbit, and changing ocean currents, the global temperature since the 1970s has risen extremely quickly. Glaciers worldwide are retreating, and in the past ten years sea levels have risen at twice the rate they did in the last century. Computer models of the climate show that the rapid warming cannot be explained by natural causes alone. Scientists are working to find ways to stop the release of heat-trapping pollution, and prevent an even hotter future.

3 — Sanger, David E., "We can't stop the hackers," published in *The New York Times,* Sunday June 17, 2018.

4 — Levitsky, Steven & Daniel Ziblatt, How *Democracies Die: What History Reveals about our Future.* (New York, Crown Publishing Group, 2018).

5 — Singer, Mark, *Trump and Me,* Crown Publishing, 2016. The author, who writes of their time together, says that Trump said to him, "You know what I consider ideal company: a total piece of ass."

6 — Fisher, Roger and Ury, William. *Getting to Yes: Negotiating Agreement Without Giving In,* (New York, Houghton Mifflin Company, 1981).

7 — Sommers, Christina Hoff, "The Gender Gage Rap is Real!" The Wall Street Journal, Thursday, March 15, 2018.

# Chapter 14

# Dangerous Convictions...

*There is no more certain sign of a narrow mind, of*
*stupidity, and of arrogance, than to stand aloof from*
*those who think differently from you.*
                    Cicero

Religious conviction has throughout history been the impetus for selfless sacrifice. It has also been the cause of malicious bloodshed. When conviction becomes uncompromising it is capable of defying credible evidence. It refuses to consider new information which could be in conflict with its tenants. It becomes part of an individual's identity. To attack one's convictions is to attack who he is.

Our religious convictions are often based on exclusivity, determining our identity through our differences. Historically, the followers of Judaism, Islam, Catholicism, and Protestantism have compartmentalized their identities to include only those of their own creed, consistent with their respective theological doctrine. Once we commit to an exclusive tribal identity, religious conviction can become divisive, suspicious and distrustful of those outside our own limited circle of faith. Instead of searching for our common humanity (our relatedness), unquestioning conviction promotes divisiveness and causes us to become resentful of those who differ from us.

My father, a staunchly pious Protestant minister, feared in the 1960s that the election of a Roman Catholic president (John Kennedy) might taint the Protestant, doctrinal principles of our founding fathers. Might it be possible for papal leverage to influence the nation's character, as had been the case in previous centuries in Europe? This was not an uncommon suspicion between Protestants and Roman Catholics in the mid-twentieth century, the days of nascent ecumenism.

When we get cozy with our God we convince ourselves that (s)he favors the same people that we do, and opposes the same ones we do. The vanity of our conviction can betray us. We stray from the teachings of the Jewish carpenter when we deny the vastness and diversity of creation. Saint Paul's exhortation to "be transformed by the renewing of your mind" becomes an uncomfortable message. We look for affirmation of our suppositions, not the renewal of our minds.

A cardiac physician in Texas posted a picture of a US president and his wife on Facebook with an accompanying message that spoke of the dignity with which the president guided our country. The message appealed to my friend's opinion of that president. But it struck an ugly nerve with some individuals who were apparently incapable of accepting the fact that anyone could hold a political opinion different from their own. The reaction was sharp and critical, evidence of self-righteous narcissism. The indignant responses showed a level of intolerance revealing how emotionally invested individuals become in their point of view. "You've got to be shitting me," one wrote. A consulting psychiatrist responded sarcastically, "You can think, work, and understand logic?!" I would not recommend this psychiatrist to anyone searching for equanimity or peace of mind. It was a picture of President Obama and his wife. The same statements could have been expressed by the other side if it had been a picture of Donald Trump and Melania. Beliefs can become an intolerant teacher when they are guided by emotion rather than reason. Challenges to our beliefs create a sense of uncomfortable insecurity, causing us to cling to them ever more strenuously.

"We *believe* in the absence of knowledge or complete assurance. Hence the quest for certainty has always been an effort to transcend belief."[1] American philosopher John Dewey wrote that we would be less inclined to self-deception if we thought of our beliefs as probability rather than certainty. He points out the distinction between knowledge and belief, or as John Locke put it, between knowledge and judgment. The former (knowledge) seeks validation through objective observation. Beliefs (judgments) can be reached in the absence of knowledge or complete assurance. In Greek philosophy belief was a lower degree of knowledge.

Beliefs can blind us to the potential truth of world views other than our own. They destroy the attempt to find common values. We become uncomfortable with anyone who does not mirror our own beliefs; we may even condemn them. The mental response of least resistance is to ridicule the person whose opinion is different from our own.

*English journalist and author G.K. Chesterton understood the need for humility and self-restraint. When he was asked to respond to a newspaper series on the question, "What is the problem in the universe?" he answered, "I am."*

Neurologist Dr. Oliver Sacks pointed out in his posthumously published book *The River of Consciousness*[2], that the brain, unlike other human organs, has no sense organ. Our nervous system monitors every other organ in our body. When the heart beats too fast, we can sense it. When we eat too much, we get a stomach ache. But our brain does not warn us when our beliefs are misguided, or when we lose cognitive functioning, develop Alzheimers, or adopt bizarre behavior. We may not be aware of our mental deterioration until some outsider warns us. (And then we may be likely to take offense!)

The force of irrational thinking can have life threatening consequences. A worker was accidently locked into a refrigeration box car used for transporting frozen foods. The crew did not notice his absence and went home for the night. When the man realized he was locked in the box car, he began banging on the door until his fists were bloody. He screamed for help until he was hoarse and lost his voice. Fear terrorized his mind as he realized he was going to freeze to death. With a pocket knife he carved a last message into the wood floor of the boxcar. "It's cold. Body getting numb. If only I could sleep. These are my last words." Next morning the man's body was discovered inside the refrigerated box car. Physical signs indicated that he could have died from hypothermia. Only one thing puzzled the investigators. The refrigeration unit on the box car was inoperative. The temperature inside the car had not fallen below the outside temperature of thirty degrees Fahrenheit. It was his inner conviction, the power of his mind that led to cardiac arrest.

The certitude with which we hold fast to a supposition can be deadly to ourselves and others. We may cling to our religious tenets to the point of violence against those who should dare to defy them. Ideology, no matter how innocent or non-violent, can incite rage and a paroxysm of revenge, diminishing the value of human life. Medieval Christians persecuted and burned religious dissenters. The leaders of the Western church believed that religious orthodoxy must be defended and safeguarded; those who opposed the teachings of scripture were believed to deserve severe punishment, even death: a scholar who doubted the doctrine of the Trinity was burned to death under John Calvin in the sixteenth century.

### Divided We Fall

Most of us search social media for affirmation, not information. We read with a particular purpose in mind, and often that purpose isn't to absorb information, but to gather evidence that champions our presumptions. Cognitive scientist Alexandra Horowitz has studied how our brains are conditioned to pay attention to information that confirms our beliefs. "Attention is an intentional, unapologetic discriminator...it gears us up to notice only what is relevant to our current perception of reality," she writes. Our minds carefully monitor the messages we receive, discriminating between what is acceptable and what is offensive to our preconceived notion.

If I should comment to an anonymous group of people that "Prayer is an effective defense against accidents and illness," some would nod in agreement. Others might shake their heads in dissent. The same is true of a statement in support of a political person: "Donald Trump is a genius who is bringing sanity back to our foreign policy." That statement would bring diametrically opposed reactions from two individuals who otherwise might interpret reality the same way. William James wrote that "Our normal waking consciousness is but one special type of consciousness, whilst all about it, parted from it by the filmiest of screens, there lie potential forms of consciousness entirely different."

Today we face in our country a conflicted citizenry, more diverse than existed at the time the Constitution was written. We are no longer united by a common heritage or a common language. We are divided by culture and religion. The gap between the rich and the poor is staggering and continues to grow wider.

"Democracy never lasts long. It soon wastes, exhausts and murders itself," John Adams wrote in 1814. "Democracy requires trust and cooperation as well as competition... we must find a way to see citizens on the other side as cousins who are sometimes opponents but who share most of our values and interests and are never our mortal enemies."

The Founding Fathers realized how tenuous their newly drafted Constitution was. They were less optimistic than many of today's defenders. In a speech before the Constitutional Convention, Benjamin Franklin said, "...when you assemble a number of men to have the advantage of their joint wisdom, you inevitably assemble with those men all their prejudices, their passions, their errors of opinion, their local interests, and their selfish views." It's no wonder Franklin responded to a group of citizens who asked what kind of government the delegates had created: "We've given you a republic...if you can keep it."

It would behoove each of us to be more self-critical, to invite more skepticism into our thought process, to challenge our beliefs. As our country becomes more politically divided, it is increasingly difficult to find common values, or any middle ground. Statements in opposition to our emotionally attached convictions are immediately offensive to us. We become stubborn, uncompromising, and filled with contempt for those who have a different political opinion. Arguments are based on emotions and personal opinion, rather than fact or policy issues.

"I like President Trump because he tells it like it is."

"I don't like President Trump because he's an idiot."

Neither of these typical statements contains objective evidence, yet neither speaker would be likely to consider contrary evidence. Beliefs are held with stubborn emotion. Our conscious minds are constantly filtering what we see and hear. We dismiss whatever challenges our emotionally held convictions. If our political discussions were confined to facts and policy debates, fewer words would be spoken.

We could improve civil discourse simply by listening patiently to opposing arguments. Maybe our intransigence contains some inconsistency. "To improve is to change. To be perfect is to change often," Winston Churchill said. Perhaps the simple act of listening is the change that would bring us closer together.

Religious practice today inspires more division than compassion. What are the grounds upon which our religious commitment is based? Can we find common ground with a Hindu, a Buddhist, a Jainist, or a Muslim? Surely we should be able to listen to each other without rancor, difficult as that may be. Skepticism is a valuable attribute to warn us that the search for truth is not the same as a search for certainty. Scottish philosopher David Hume wrote that truth is not an absolute, metaphysical certainty.

John Adams, in a speech to the military in 1798, warned his fellow countrymen, "We have no government armed with power capable of contending with human passions unbridled by morality and religion...Our Constitution was made only for a moral and religious people. It is wholly inadequate to the government of any other."

✠ ✠ ✠

When our beliefs become ingrained in our self-perception, we dismiss the most obvious evidence. "Help me understand why you believe that," is not a quest we readily pursue when someone opposes our point of view. We look for the information that confirms what has become identified with who we are. The ability to consider that "I may be wrong," requires humility and self-awareness. It reveals an inner security, an ability to grow, to expand, to evolve, and to occupy a new space beyond stagnation. Skepticism protects me from gullibility. It also prompts self-examination, and fends off self-righteous judgment.

Analysts claim that the hunger for affirmation is the result of insecurity — the need for personal reassurance. There is neurological evidence which indicates that once our minds are made up, we resist changing despite any evidence. We see ourselves as insightful individuals, who analyze the facts before we form an opinion. We resist any evidence that might contradict what we believe. Our final decision-making is processed through the amygdala, the emotion center of the brain. We believe what we want to believe, facts be damned. We continue to get our news exclusively from those sources that satisfy our emotional needs and provide affirmation rather than information.

No one reasons with pure logic. Our brains receive mental images of the world around us. But the mind interprets on a narrow canvas what the brain perceives. The mind connects our thinking to the heart and emotions. Our emotions dictate our responses. If a person operated with pure logic, he might be a heartless beast. But emotions often deceive us. We stop listening; we over-react or become unnecessarily defensive.

The philosophy of ethical determinism taught that to *know* what is good (what is the socially acceptable, proper thing to do) provided the necessary impetus to *do* what was good. This was the philosophy of Plato, who optimistically believed that knowledge guides conduct. All we need to do is make sure everyone *knows* what the good is. But *knowing* doesn't guarantee *doing* in human behavior. In this case the New Testament seems to have had more insight into human character than the Greek philosopher. Saint Paul confessed his own limitation: "For I do not do the good I want to do, but the evil I do not want to do — this I keep doing."

✠ ✠ ✠

Religious practices differ from one culture to another. Sacrificing animals on an altar is animal cruelty in most countries. In others it is a sacred religious act. "Normal" in one person's mind may be considered an aberration or mental disorder in another cultural setting. The fact that normal is not a permanent, stationary condition, is evident when we refer to the "new normal" or when we learn about strange customs throughout the world that to us may seem irrational. Our minds are capable of deceiving us, often in the strangest ways.

In parts of Japan and Russia, the Ainu people have a custom of sacrificing bears. They believe that the bears are gods and to sacrifice them shows a sign of religious devotion. We believe this practice is inhumane: it involves killing a hibernating mother bear in her cave, raising her cubs in captivity for two years, then choking or spearing them as a sign of religious devotion. The villagers drink the blood of the bear. They eat the flesh and place the skull on a spear which becomes a focal point of worship. This is a devout spiritual practice for the Ainu people. To us, it is gruesome and irrational.

The Toraja people of Indonesia perform a ritual of digging up the corpses of their fellow villagers, whether they are adults or children and whether the death was recent or decades old. They dress the corpse in special clothing and parade it around the village. The intention is to cleanse the corpse and ceremoniously return it to the home village, symbolizing the act of returning home. That is perfectly normal if you're a Toraja.

What might be normal in one culture could be viewed as ludicrous, even harmful, in another. Consuming seventy-two hot dogs to achieve a prize may seem like light-hearted competition to some and suicidal gluttony to others. When worshippers walk to an altar to drink a cup of wine and eat a morsel of bread, claiming ceremoniously that it is the body and blood of God, they consider it to be a normal spiritual worship ritual. Other cultures who hear of it for the first time think it is abnormal. They claim it sounds like cannibalism. Then again normal is a slippery word. As someone said, the only normal people are the ones you don't know very well.

So what is normal? Even in the field of psychiatry there is no clear answer to that question. There is a wide range of behavior that can simply be diagnosed as anxiety, forgetfulness, poor habits, or eccentricity.

Dr. Allen Frances is a professor emeritus and former chair of the Department of Psychiatry and Behavioral Science at Duke University School of Medicine. He has written the book *Saving Normal*[3],which warns that medical science is over-reaching in its tendency to label everyday human responses as mental disorders, and then prescribe unnecessary treatment.

The bible of psychiatry, a manual entitled *Diagnostic and Statistical Manual,* describes hundreds of possible mental disorders, many of which are simply common responses to the stress of coping with daily problems. Every few years it is updated, resulting in more "mental patients," a case of diagnostic hyperinflation.

Dr. Frances realized that with each new edition there were many more so-called disorders that would create millions of new "patients." This diagnostic inflation was opening the door for too many people becoming dependent on doctor prescribed medication for every day anxiety, sleeping problems, and pain.

Normal is not easy to pin down. Conduct that is considered normal or socially acceptable floats along a wide continuum of human behavior. Social norms change from culture to culture, from country to country, from north to south. In Japan it is not appropriate to give a tip. In Saudi Arabia it is rude to blow your nose in public. In northern Spain men run and jump over infants who are laid out on mattresses to scare away the devil. And in our country it is customary to observe the behavior of a groundhog to determine how long winter will last. Before we become experts at diagnosing others, it behooves us to monitor our own behavior. Before we pass judgment on a person whose religious practice or political affiliation differs from our own, we are wise to pause and consider with a degree of awe and appreciation the wide diversity of human thought and behavior. If we don't, we become self-righteous critics of anyone who doesn't behave as we do, think as we do, or look like us. "Normal," writes Dr. Frances, "has been badly besieged and is already sadly diminished. Dictionaries can't provide a satisfying definition; philosophers argue over its meaning; statisticians and psychologists measure it endlessly, but fail to capture its essence…and doctors of the mind and body are busily nipping away at its borders."4

I continue to maintain a healthy degree of skepticism. I strive to widen the lens of my perception about others as well as myself. Before I denounce, I will ask "Why?"

## Notes

1 — Dewey, John. *The Quest for Certainty: A Study of the Relation of Knowledge and Action.* (New York, G.P. Putnam's Sons, c. 1929.) p. 26.

2 — Sachs, Oliver. *The River of Consciousness.* (New York, Alfred A. Knopf, 2017).

3 — Frances, Allen. *Saving Normal.* (New York, Harper Collins, 2013) p. 61 f.

4 — Ibid, p.3

Chapter 15

# How Normal Are You?

*What we call normal in psychology is really a psychopathology of the average, so undramatic and so widely spread that we don't even notice it ordinarily.*
Abraham Maslow

At its peak in the 1950s over 7,000 patients were held in the overcrowded Elgin Illinois Mental Institution. As an intern, living within the walls of that facility for several months, I interviewed individuals afflicted with a wide range of diagnosed mental disorders. Elias (not his real name) was certain that his wife had been replaced by an alien, or an imposter. When she came to visit him at the institution, he swore at her; he told her to get away from him and never to come back to see him. She was heart-broken to be so bitterly scorned after almost forty years of marriage. I learned that this rare disorder was called *Capgras* syndrome, named after a French psychiatrist who first described it in 1923. Elias was so terrified of this woman that he responded with rage when I attempted to persuade him that she was his wife. He became violent and resentful of me.

Another unusual patient, Eloise (not her real name), suffered from a rare form of dementia. I was told to monitor her closely, because she would crawl on the ground and eat grass and weeds. When I approached her she would make a mooing sound like a cow. Although it appeared to be a childish game, I was told by the doctor that it was a diagnosed mental disorder; and yes, it had a name known in psychiatry as *boanthropy*. This mental disorder was mentioned in the Old Testament Book of Daniel, where it is claimed that Nebuchadnezzar II, the king of the Babylonian Empire in 605 BC was humbled by God for boasting about his achievements. As a result he lost his sanity and lived like an animal for seven years.

Each of us perceives the world about us in a distinctive way. The basic sensory perceptions — sight, taste, touch, smell, and hearing — can differ from one person to the next. I may look at a painting and see a beautiful image. Another person might see a sloppy attempt to create a landscape. I eat a banana and delight in its taste and softness. My wife can't stand the mushy texture. A friend loves modern jazz music. I hear cacophony and an undisciplined series of notes. When this continuum of human perception reaches the outer limits, it leads to behavior that is far distant from what we consider "normal." When that happens those individuals are often confined in an institution which protects them from themselves and others.

## Think You Are Normal? Don't Be Too Sure

The human brain has the capacity to create an imaginary microcosm that may have little connection to reality, or the world perceived by the five senses.

Dr. Giulio Tononi, professor of psychiatry and neuroscience at the University of Wisconsin-Madison, explains that the brain has pathways through which signals are transmitted. Like a highway, the signals can go in two directions: information can be incoming from the senses, while other outward bound signals are initiated by the imagination from memories and emotional sensations.[1]

The power of the imagination has the ability to form a mental image that is not perceived through the five senses. The mind can create scenes or events that do not exist. An entire world prevails within the mind. Some individuals have highly developed imaginations. They are the creative types who can mold their own world apart from either moral norms or perceived reality.

When we consider this diversity in human sense perception, along with distinctive memories and imagination of each person, it is no wonder that it is so difficult to achieve religious or political consensus. Two individuals may look at the same politician or the same religious creed and reach opposite judgments.

The power of imagination is one of the most potent human characteristics and can be employed to achieve personal goals. Everyone has the ability to use his or her imagination to improve self-confidence or develop a skill. Motivational affirmations are used by high achievers to reach a goal.

*I never give up.*

*I live each day to the fullest.*

*I am an intelligent person.*

Studies have shown, however, that positive affirmations are more effective when an individual uses his own name. For example, instead of "I never give up," one would say, "Joe never gives up," (using his own name.) When Henry decided to become more health conscious and lose weight, he was able to keep to his plan more successfully by employing the affirmation, 'Henry stops eating before he is filled.' When Susan was trying to finish a marathon, she discovered she could pull out more inner reserve of endurance when she said, 'Susan can finish this race,' rather than 'I can finish this race.'

A Swedish study by Christopher Berger, a doctoral student at the Department of Neuroscience, demonstrated that our imagination can distort the way we hear a sound or see a shape. Some people literally see the world through rose-colored glasses. Others see a dark cloud over every condition and a dire warning in every event. The value of skepticism lies in its constant whisper, 'Don't be too sure.'

*Jesus said it. I believe it. That settles it.*
(Bumper sticker)

In the Peanuts cartoon, Snoopy informs Linus that he is writing a theology book. He has decided that the title will be "Has It Ever Occurred To You That You Might Be Wrong?" This is the humble posture appropriate for anyone who is "seeking truth."

I achieve the best mental and emotional balance when I am listening, learning, and self-questioning, because no matter how much I may resist acknowledging it, 'I might be wrong.'

The human intellect draws upon past experience and deeply felt emotions. The mind is capable of a wide range of delusions which affect judgment and perception. When we acknowledge this fact we become less tied to the intractable insistence of accepting nothing but our own judgment. We become better listeners when we attempt to respond with more compassion and less condemnation. Skepticism enables us to be less gullible. It gives us the courage to challenge our own suppositions.

I call myself a skeptic because it provides a safety zone between reality and delusion. When I become insecure I flee to the safety of certitude. It is more comforting to reach a conclusion, to have the certainty of an answer. Finding truth is more satisfying than seeking truth. But skepticism issues the ever constant warning to be careful, you might be wrong.

Imagination and memory can deceive us, as we will see in the following pages. Our minds create a cacophony of neural signals, altering our perceptions of reality.

A catalogue of mental disorders[2] lists over one hundred fifty from A (*Agoraphobia* — irrational fear of enclosed, public places) to X (*Xenophobia* — dislike or distrust of people who don't speak your language or are from other countries.) Search through the list of phobias and you may find a description that sounds a little like yourself. For every normal emotional experience, there is a more extreme version which becomes classified as a phobia or form of mental illness. You may dislike spiders, but if your fear becomes a bit excessive, there is a name for you in the psychiatric journal: *arachnophobe*.

Behaviors with the suffix "-philia" indicate the opposite of a phobia. They are categorized under the heading of *paraphylias*, and indicate erotic attraction to unusual situations or individuals. The American Psychiatric Association lists over 100 of them.

*Necrophylia* is the erotic attraction to corpses. (The opposite, or fear of corpses, is called *necrophobia.) Acrotomophilia* indicates an erotic interest in people with amputations. *Pedophilia* is a more commonly used term, indicating an unhealthy erotic attraction to children. We are all attracted to babies, but an unhealthy, chronic obsession with infants is called *infantophilia*. This mental disorder has incited infant kidnapping.

*Pygophilia* describes an individual with an extremely erotic interest focused on the buttocks; and usually the bigger, the better.

A less egregious mental condition is *sophophilia*, an erotic zeal for learning and pedantry. (I could not have been accused of this during my college years.)

In our country the second amendment provides government support for the right to own a gun. When possession of firearms becomes an obsession, it is diagnosed as *hoplophilia*.

Then there are the disorders with the suffix "-lagnia." *Aniliagnia* is the sexual attraction by young men to older women. *Hematolagnia* indicates an erotic desire to drink or look at blood.

Did you ever find yourself in the company of someone who wanted to smell your armpits? Seriously, it happens. Psychiatrists diagnose this disorder as *maschalagnia*.

My wife occasionally points out someone who is dressed inappropriately; often it's an older man or woman who likes to imagine that he or she is still a grade-schooler. If someone comes to work dressed in short shorts, a white ruffled shirt and cute little bow tie and baseball cap, and it reminds you of yourself when you were six years old, he is possibly suffering from *pedovestism*. You may start looking more closely at how your co-workers are dressed.

By now most of us would be thinking how fortunate we are not to be afflicted with these aberrations of behavior. Maybe we are normal, we think to ourselves. Don't be too sure. The more we learn about strange behavior, the more needful it is to be self-aware, to be less judgmental.

You may be a typical romantic. Carried to the extreme is the individual who falls in love too easily, and with too many people — a form of sexual addiction, which can lead to stalking and the delusion that the unknowing victim being stalked is in love with the addict.

You may have firmly held Christian convictions. Those convictions can be employed in the service of humanitarian sacrifice or turned into fanatical self-righteous vindictiveness, readiness to pass judgment rather than bestow compassion.

Some phobic disorders can emerge as a normal response to the stress of contemporary living. In 2008, the term *nomophobia* (short for no-mobile phobia) was coined in the UK to describe the anxiety some people experience when they are out of mobile contact or realize they have 5% battery life remaining. In the last four years over a dozen papers have been published about smart phone addiction and the treatments available for the fears and anxieties that are created by smart-phone related usage. Retreat spaces, called "7 % rooms" have been created for people who become panic stricken when they discover they have only 7 % battery power remaining on their mobile phones.

A quirk or peculiarity could be found in any one of us if we were measured against one of the many psychiatric barometers listed in medical texts. Before we pass judgment or demand too much conformity of others, we must admit that someone who is absolutely "normal" might also be utterly boring. Idiosyncrasy, whimsy, and non-conformity are the qualities that forge interesting characters. An intelligent awareness of the range of human needs, desires, and emotional cravings should guide us toward tolerance, even as it encourages us to be self-aware, perhaps even self-critical.

Spiritual guidance should encourage compassion for all beings. But even religious tolerance has its limits, as this amusing story illustrates:

A woman and her grandmother, a very forgiving, religious soul, are sitting on the porch discussing another member of the family. "He's no good," the young woman says. "He's completely untrustworthy, not to mention lazy."

"Yes, he's bad," grandmother says as she rocks back and forth. "But Jesus loves him."

"I'm not so sure about that," the young woman answers.

"Oh yes, Jesus loves him." Grandmother continues to rock in deep thought for a moment, and then adds, "Of course Jesus doesn't know him like we do."

✛ ✛ ✛

Some mental perceptions are beyond our comprehension. Body Integrity Identity Disorder (BIID) is a condition in which the individual has an intense desire to amputate a major limb or sever the spinal cord in order to become paralyzed. Also referred to as *Xenomelia*, it is the oppressive sensation that one or more limbs of one's body don't belong to one's self. There were such individuals living in the hospital where I worked. As an unskilled intern, I was unable to do anything more than listen to these individuals and attempt to understand the world in which they lived, while trying to prevent them from harming themselves. It proved to me that the mind is capable of dramatic deception and we should all be aware of the need for constant surveillance to determine how accurately we ourselves are interpreting the outside world and the people who surround us; to ask ourselves the question, "Did it ever occur to you that you might be wrong?"

There is nothing as disarming as talking to a person who, during fifteen minutes of conversation, sounds and appears normal in every way, until you suddenly discover that he is the reincarnated Christ...or so he is convinced.

Living on the grounds of this mental hospital for several months with its eerie night sounds and daily companionship with delusional humanity, I felt at times as though I was at risk of becoming one of them. The history of our management of the mentally and criminally insane has included barbaric treatment, exacerbating the condition which required confinement in the first place. Many of the underpaid attendants at the facility had migrated from small towns of southern states. They had no training in the care of mental illnesses and no comprehension of what mental illness was all about. Some of the younger female attendants, who worked in the worst wards of the hospital where the severely delusional patients were held, antagonized male patients, provocatively exposing themselves to the men confined in cells. They laughed at and taunted the confused men, who masturbated in response to the mocking girls. The few trained medical personnel were so overwhelmed with administrative duties that they were not involved with actual patient care.

One of the young female attendants asked me if I would like to attend a party with her at an apartment in Chicago. I knew the invitation was offered only because she needed a ride for the one and a half hour drive to downtown Chicago.

When we arrived on the eighth floor of a non-descript building south of the loop, we walked into a smoke-filled apartment where a group of about twenty-five university students, who called themselves political organizers, were sitting in a circle on the floor around the periphery of a room that was devoid of any furniture. I sat and listened for two hours as they discussed how they were going to carry out a protest the next day against various government agencies. Gradually the group broke up, with some leaving and others falling into a drug-induced sleep in other rooms. I lay down on a couch and tried to sleep for an hour and then decided to find my passenger to tell her I was going to return to Elgin. After looking into a couple dimly lit rooms without finding her, I opened a door to one last room. My passenger looked up in surprise. She was naked and lying head-to-crotch with another female. My theological education and awareness of human nature was broadened with these doses of earthy reality.

A decade or so after I left the Elgin State Hospital, it was almost closed down; those who were not considered a danger to themselves or others were turned out on the streets, increasing by thousands the number of helpless and homeless individuals camped out in parks and underpasses across the country.

Witnessing the hard-headed certainty with which these patients of Elgin State Hospital held to their convictions about the world around them, left me with a lasting awareness of the need for constant vigilance to remain in search of truth, realizing that it will always exist just beyond my grasp.

## Notes

1 — Dr. Guilio Tononi is a neuroscientist and psychiatrist at the University of Wisconsin. He has conducted extensive studies in the function of sleep, and is a leader in the field of consciousness studies. Books authored and co-authored include:

Tononi, Guilio, *PHI: A Voyage from the Brain to the Soul,* Pantheon Books, 2012.

Laureys, S., Tononi, Guilio, *The Neurology of Consciousness: Cognitive Neuroscience and Neuropathology,* Academic Press, 2009.

Edelman, G.M., Tononi, Guilio, *A Universe of Consciousness: How Matter Becomes Imagination,* Basic Books, 2000.

Sporns, O., Tononi, Guilio, *Selectionism and the Brain,* Academic Press, 1994

2 — The American Psychiatric Association's standard reference for psychiatry includes over 450 different definitions of mental disorders: *The Diagnostic and Statistical Manual of Mental Disorders (DSM).*

3 — Emerson, Ralph Waldo. From an essay on *Self Reliance,* 1841.

# Chapter 16

# Duel To The Death

*What ardently we wish we soon believe.*
Edward Young, d. 1765

Early in our nation's history, political disputes were settled with gun duels when they couldn't be resolved by debate or compromise. At a time when most northern states were starting to outlaw the practice, it was still carried out in the south. Refusing to accept the challenge to a duel could mark the end of a political career. One of the most famous duels in our country's history was between Vice President Aaron Burr and Alexander Hamilton, who had served as Secretary of the Treasury. The duel took place in 1804 and resulted in the killing of Hamilton. It marked the culmination of a skirmish between the Democratic-Republicans and the Federalists. (The balance in the US Treasury at that time was $5,800,000, about $2 million less than the government spends per minute today.)

Two years later future president Andrew Jackson killed Charles Dickinson in a duel, after Dickinson had cheated him on a horse race bet and insulted his wife. The duel had no effect on Jackson's campaign for the presidency in 1829. Jackson may have participated in as many as 100 duels.

Mark Twain became embroiled in a dispute with a newspaper editor. It was so rancorous that Mark Twain challenged the editor to a duel, but then passed out in terror before it could take place.

The method of settling political disputes in our country has gone through a long history of development, attempting to settle differences through conciliation, mediation, and negotiation. Thankfully, these eventually took the place of fatal gun duels.

✠ ✠ ✠

It was Mark Twain who wrote that "Travel is fatal to prejudice, bigotry, and narrow-mindedness." Experiencing other cultures broadens our understanding of human nature and reduces our fear and suspicion of those who are different from us. Skepticism encourages us to keep an open mind, even to the point of challenging time-honored traditions...like gun duels.

Psychological studies have documented the connection between prejudice and lack of association or familiarity. I grew up in a small, Midwestern town near the Mississippi River. The 2,800 inhabitants of the community were white and politically conservative. I don't know if I held any prejudice against minorities because I had not been around any. I was vaguely aware that my devout parents found any form of bigotry objectionable. But I never had a chance to find out my own personal reaction to ethnic diversity, because there were no minorities in any of the public schools in our village. It wasn't until I attended college in a city 500 miles away that I experienced an ethnically diverse student community. While there must have been ample evidence of bigotry in the 1960s, I was not aware that it had a bearing on my college friendships.

In retrospect, I realize that my fraternity was segregated, but I had no reservations about dating a female of a different color. Many of my friendships with football and basketball players included black students. The ethnic differences simply seemed irrelevant to me, although I'm sure they were just under the surface.

Mark Twain might have added that familiarity, like travel, is also fatal to prejudice. Often our suspicions about others are kindled by lack of knowledge. We are wary of the unfamiliar. My mother was convinced that anyone who came from Russia was an untrustworthy communist. That opinion changed when she was forced to share a room with a Russian woman on a ship to Europe sixty years ago. As it turned out, the woman was a devout Christian, as are 50%

of the people of Russia. She and my mother developed a warm friendship, despite the language barrier. Familiarity banished the uninformed misjudgment.

A young boy from a sheltered all-white high school in Ohio discovered the common humanity he shared with a black student when he was placed in the same university dorm room. In both these situations, prejudice was displaced by closeness and familiarity.

A stranger seen from afar can be frightening. When we get up close and personal we experience the commonalities of our humanity. Skepticism encourages self-examination. It compels us to question naïve assumptions.

## Belief Is A Lower Form Of Knowledge

Personal conviction often resists opposing evidence, leaving no room for growth or learning. Members of the Flat Earth Society, founded in 1956, promote the idea that the Earth is flat rather than a sphere, despite scientific evidence. Those who are serious about this claim are motivated by religious literalism.

Some individuals believe that human activity has no effect on global warming, despite evidence published by a large majority of climate scientists. Their claims are made as personal judgments, unrelated to objective reality. They may take pride in their resistance to the factual evidence. Beliefs that are held in defiance of scientific evidence are often maintained as identity badges, bold evidence of personal independence.

Conviction provides the comfort of security. Doubt is associated with losing control. It is discomforting to hear evidence that disputes our beliefs. Our knee-jerk response is to reject what conflicts with our convictions. Furthermore, we resent those who bring up evidence that challenges our beliefs.

I listened to a teenage boy who defiantly claimed, "My dad says human activity has no effect on global warming and I believe that too." He takes his stand as a loyalty oath to his father. Filial loyalty supersedes intellectual curiosity.

Such conviction makes it too painful to consider evidence contrary to what his father has told him. Bigotry, likewise, is passed on from generation to generation. Beliefs become badges of tribal identity: my family, my gang, or the guys with whom I hang out. We feel uncomfortable with those who hold contrary beliefs. The boy's intransigence indicates that the matter is settled in his world. He takes pride in his bold stand.

Beliefs maintained in defiance of evidence create barriers. They defy the common ground of observable reality. They resist a willingness to expand, to engage in the ongoing challenge of seeking truth. When we refuse to challenge our beliefs, we destroy the capacity to reach consensus or find common values. Greek philosophy counsels that belief is a lower form of knowledge.

The mind is the agency that enables us to experience our environment and make judgments about it. It is the organ by which we think and choose. In philosophical literature it is also related to a person's spirit, or psyche. It is a terrible thing to go unchallenged in the pursuit of truth. Skepticism disrupts mental stagnation in order to make room for learning. Dogmatism closes the mind to new paths of discovery.

Shortly after I was married, I described to my wife the tall fruit trees in the back yard of the home where I had grown up in Ohio. When I was five years old I climbed those trees to pick the fruit. I was afraid of falling to the ground, which was far below the branches where I sat. In my mind the branches reached high up into the sky. A few years after we were married we visited that house. I was shocked to see that the fruit trees in that back yard were only a few feet taller than I. The height of the trees had not diminished. My perception of that reality had changed. I was looking at the world from a different perspective.

Fact and reality are often distinctly unrelated in our memory. Perception becomes more accurate when it is scrutinized and challenged. When we explore beliefs that are contrary to our own, we may not change our belief, but we will enlarge our understanding of the diversity of human nature. Our first inclination is to frame our rebuttal, to prove that we are right.

There are times when we must make commitments, despite personal reservations. Purposeful living requires that we cast our lot with causes despite our doubts. We would be ineffectual, gutless, and lacking in character if we went through life without taking a stand. But wisdom bids us always to hold something in reserve when we are confronted with challenges to our commitments.

Recall how Abraham Lincoln privately admitted his doubts, while preserving his commitment to unify the country. In one of his speeches Lincoln referred to America as God's "almost chosen people."[1] This curious description, *almost chosen,* left open the debate of whether our country was on the right track. It revealed Lincoln's humility and his ardent desire to achieve peaceful co-existence, a *United* States. Before issuing an Emancipation Proclamation, Lincoln wrote to the editor of the *New York Tribune,* "My paramount object in this struggle is to save the Union, and is not either to save or destroy slavery. If I could save the Union without freeing any slave, I would do it; and if I could save it by freeing all the slaves, I would do it."[2] The depth of his turmoil is evidenced in this statement. By revealing this internal struggle he showed more strength of character than one who might autocratically dictate only one side without showing empathy for the serious considerations of both sides. Nonetheless, on January 1, 1863, President Lincoln issued the Emancipation Proclamation granting federal legal status to more than 3.5 million enslaved African Americans in ten states.

Skepticism prevented Lincoln from associating with any specific religious creed. However, his writings reveal a profound faith. His reverential acceptance address at the Second Inaugural was imbued with humility. Consider the poetic eloquence of his speech:

"With malice toward none; with charity for all; with firmness in the right, as God gives us the right, let us strive on to finish the work we are in; to bind up the nation's wounds; to care for him who shall have borne the battle, and for his widow, and his orphan — to do all which may achieve and cherish a just and lasting peace among ourselves, and with all nations."

While skepticism has brought grief and turmoil to the minds of history's great leaders, it has not prevented them from committing themselves to bold action when circumstances required it. Wise leadership unifies. Ineffective leaders divide.

The humble statement of Abraham Lincoln stands in bold contrast to the arrogance and narcissism of contemporary political statements.

Institutions of learning should teach the art of listening, which leads to a more successful conclusion than futile argumentation. In the book *Power Listening: Mastering the Most Critical Business Skill of All*[3], author Bernard Ferrari writes that the refusal or inability to listen is at the root of most bad decisions. Executives are fired and products fail when listening is overpowered by the desire to foist an opinion on others. Managers who admit to some uncertainty, who ask questions and welcome suggestions, receive more support and loyalty from their employees. Workers take greater pride in their careers when their views are welcomed by a boss, even if they are contrary to his management. When the boss recognizes that he is not infallible — he is more highly respected and creates a cohesive workforce.

Doctors take too little time listening to patients. Research studies have shown that in consultation with their patients, doctors do most of the talking and often make diagnoses too quickly. Doctors and surgeons who are overly confident and dogmatically certain about their diagnoses make a higher percentage of errors. As the day progresses and doctors grow more tired they tend to order unnecessary tests, "just to be safe." (Studies have shown that doctors write more prescriptions in afternoon appointments, a simpler default conclusion than asking more questions and engaging in a longer appointment.) It has been estimated that $200 billion is wasted in the US annually on over-treatment of tests and medications.[4] Doctors who are the most certain about their diagnoses make the most mistakes. We should be more inclined to trust the doctor who says, "I'm not sure."

Jamie Holmes in the book *Nonsense: The Power of Not Knowing* has written about how dismayingly common medical misdiagnoses are. He describes the case of a 52-year-old woman who discovered a golf ball sized lump on her torso. It was removed by a surgeon and sent to two labs for analysis. The results that came back appeared to be conclusive: a rare form of incurable cancer and a maximum of six months to live.

The woman was skeptical because she had no physical systems of pain or side effects. She decided to review the detailed medical reports and discovered that neither one seemed clearly defined. One said 'most suspicious for.' She went to a new doctor who ordered another biopsy. The report that came back was 'no sign of malignancy.'

The misdiagnosis caused her to suffer weeks of emotional distress. And she found after doing more research that her case was common. As many as 98,000 Americans die each year because of medical errors caused by doctors taking too little time to discuss the problem with their patients or to listen to what the patient is saying.[5]

A test study of doctors who estimated the probability of streptococcal infection of patients who had come to them with colds showed that they had overestimated by 81% the probability of a positive culture. Their treatment decisions were decided upon accordingly.[6]

For listening to be effective among our social relationships, a participant in a conversation should attempt to speak no more than half the time. An educated mind is open to exploring differences before reaching a conclusion. A skeptic continues to analyze his own suppositions, as diligently as he does those of others. Sadly, we avoid difficult topics with friends when we know we have radically different opinions. Or we simply have nothing to do with those individuals, finding it too painful to hear what they say. We forsake the hard work of listening.

A young student at Williams College organized a group called "Uncomfortable learning." The group invites speakers who present controversial ideas and viewpoints. In the process students learn the futility of emotional rant, as opposed to the skill of listening and persuasive argumentation.

Peggy Noonan wrote in the editorial *Declarations*, that "rage is a poor fuel in politics. It produces a heavy, sulfurous exhaust and pollutes the air...It has many powers but not the power to persuade."[7]

Right wing conservatives can test their objectivity and emotional fortitude by watching CNN or MSNBC. Likewise, liberals should invest a portion of their news-watching time on the Fox News channel. Each side becomes more aware of their own biases when they search for the common ground.

If we are confident about our ability to think independently, we will spend as much time as necessary listening to and understanding those who think differently. We test the validity of our beliefs; we clarify our own thinking, and hone our skill of clear-headed discourse. Others are more likely to be persuaded when we speak with the calm power of persuasion.

The first century B.C. Roman philosopher Cicero, advised that happiness can never be found by anyone who allows emotional tumult to rule his existence. He insisted that commitment to self-mastery was necessary when dealing with one's emotions. Perhaps nowhere is that more true, yet more difficult, than when engaging in discussions with a political opponent.

✠ ✠ ✠

The polarization of political views results in a widening gap that threatens our democracy. It is difficult to reach compromise, to agree on common values when rational discussion becomes impossible. The Pew Research Center reports that the percentage of those who call themselves "liberal" has almost doubled, while those who call themselves "moderates" has declined. They report that the divide occurs mostly along cultural lines: the Republicans have a majority among blue collar workers, a number that is growing. Voters with a bachelor's degree have moved in large numbers to the left. This is a reversal of traditional proponents of the left and right.

The 2016 presidential election did not offer a compelling choice for voters of either political party. This was born out by how narrow the voting between the two candidates turned out to be. Before the election a friend admitted to me, "I'm going to hold my nose and vote for..." The point is not who he voted for, but that few voters entered the polls with unwavering conviction about their choice.

History has proven that an effective politician may not be an individual of appealing character. And moral integrity does not guarantee effective political leadership. The father of modern political theory, Italian philosopher, Niccolo Machiavelli, believed that the two traits (moral integrity and political success) were incompatible.

During the Renaissance, Machiavelli wrote the famous handbook, *The Prince*[8], which became a manual for powerful rulers. "There is nothing more important than to appear religious," he wrote. Machiavelli's writings suggest that politicians can be immoral liars as long as they are sly about it. He made it clear that it is impossible to be both a good politician and a moral person.

A forceful leader should rule with "cruelty dressed up as piety," dictating with just enough disruption and threats that his subjects would fear criticizing or resisting him. Machiavelli's most distinctive proposition was his rejection of Christian virtue as a guide for leaders. Rulers cannot defend the country from external threats by being merciful and tolerant. Machiavelli wrote that ethical Christianity is based on weakness and is incompatible with good governance. He used the paradoxical phrase "criminal virtue" to describe the rule of effective leadership.

The dictatorship of Vladimir Putin is a textbook illustration of the Machiavellian dictum for achieving and retaining political power. And his manifesto rings with a familiar tone in our country's current political deliberations.

Although Machiavelli became famous for his work, *The Prince,* he failed as a politician in his time.

The disconnect between moral purity and effective presidential leadership goes back to the beginning of American history. George Washington fathered his only child with a slave girl named Venus in 1784. The story of Sally Hemmings is better known. She was the slave girl of President Thomas Jefferson. After the death of Jefferson's wife, Martha, the president fathered six children with his black mistress.

The affairs of President Kennedy with beautiful women were legendary. Most famous was his affair with Marilyn Monroe. Judith Exner claimed to have been introduced to Kennedy by Frank Sinatra after which they engaged in an eighteen month affair. She published a memoir in 1977 in which she also claimed that Kennedy would throw White House pool parties with prostitutes.

James Buchanan, president in 1857, was a rare exception. He was the only United States president to remain a bachelor throughout his life. According to historians he never showed any interest in women.

The presidency of Warren Harding in 1920 occurred at a time when spiritual piety was on the rise with the emergence of evangelists and tent preachers. New church denominations were formed during this period. Albert Simpson founded the Christian and Missionary Alliance. Pentecostalism appeared with the healing ministry of Maria Woodworth-Etter. Billy Sunday held rallies to protest alcohol consumption, which led to the Prohibition. Jerry Falwell founded Liberty University and the Moral Majority.

Ethical indiscretions were carefully hidden. Gossip flourished, but printed media revelations of sexual affairs by politicians were off-limits to the press. Hypocrisy was the rule. No politician could have qualified as a presidential contender if he had divorce in his background.

Harding's presidency was one of the shallowest and most corrupt in recent history. Elaine Weiss wrote about Harding's scandalous political career. Her editorial in the *Wall Street Journal*, June 2-3, 2018 edition, describes the actions of Harding's cabinet secretaries and advisors who enriched themselves at public expense.[9]

Weiss wrote that during Harding's ten-year political rise in Ohio, he had been carrying on an affair with a family friend and neighbor, Carrie Phillips, who was the wife of a business owner in Marion, Ohio. Their love letters revealed that Warren promised to divorce his wife and marry Carrie. Those intentions were quashed when it became evident that Harding had a chance to become president. Carrie realized that the relationship was doomed. But even more infuriating was her discovery that Randy Harding had at the same time been two-timing her in an affair with a woman less than half his age. Nan Britton had a teenage crush on Harding, with whom he fathered a daughter.

Harding, who ran on the familiar sounding campaign slogan "America First" saved his presidential candidacy by paying Carrie Phillips and her husband $25,000 ($300,000 today) if they would leave the country. They traveled to Japan, China, and Korea. They were also promised a monthly stipend of $2,000 ($25,000 today) to remain silent as long as necessary.

Harding died of a heart attack in 1923 at age 57. The weakness of his presidency included personal enrichment, bribery, and scandal. Nan Britton "lost the child support payments that he (Harding) had promised and, desperate for income, wrote an X-rated memoir of their relationship."[10]

✚ ✚ ✚

Presidents have always been subject to some of the most outrageous criticism in public media. The difference between Trump and previous presidents is that he would abolish the free press if he could. And he draws more attention to it by responding to every negative remark.

John Adams may also have wished he could eliminate the press, but he ignored the flagrant rhetoric aimed at him by the news media. The *Northumberland Gazette* made the charge that President John Adams was a "power-mad despot...and an increasingly dangerous enemy to the Republic." A pamphlet published at the time called the president "a repulsive pedant, a gross hypocrite, an unprincipled oppressor...one of the most egregious fools upon the continent." The author of that pamphlet was convicted of criminal libel and imprisoned.

I am perplexed by the unusual degree of emotion with which Trump supporters react to the slightest mention of judgment about President Trump. We have grown so terribly divided that the mere mention of the president's name drives supporters and opponents to separate corners incapable of searching for common ground, and unable to discuss whether Trump policies are good or bad. It hints at the difficulty of defending a president who leaves himself open to ridicule. When he goes off script and utters the statement, "Do you believe in the gene thing? I mean, I do," the public seems justified in questioning the level of his intelligence. But he persists, "I have great genes and all that stuff, which I'm a believer in."

He offered these words of reassurance at his campaign rally in Indiana: "See you have to understand, I have a better education than they do, from a much better school, but — the elite. They're the elite. They're the elite. I went to better schools. I went to better everything. And by the way, by the way, are you ready for this? I'm the president and they're not." That level of adolescent rhetoric is such a departure from the calm, articulate communication of previous presidents, that one cannot help feeling a bit embarrassed for him.

Close advisors and insiders have leaked fears that Trump seems to have lost touch with reality. They say that when his term ends, startling revelations of his untenable state of mind will appear. His delusions are frightening. At that Indiana rally he was quoted as saying, "We've done a great job. And we have really no laws to work with. We have really no laws to work with. The laws are horrible. Laws are the worst and dumbest in this history of the world." And near the end of his speech he stated, "And I'm not saying — I'm just saying. I'm not saying its — I'm just saying something incredible is happening with our country to have this." What *is* he saying?

As the cheers erupt, one has to ask, is he saying "it" or not? It's confusing. But he pulls them in with this: "We love winners. We love winners. Winners are winners." Is that clear enough?

The success or failure of the Trump administration is yet to be known. The validation of political success is almost always based on how well the economy fares. Regardless of who can be credited for the rise or decline of the American economy — the administration in DC or a conflation of historical events — a citizenry is ultimately influenced by their comfort and financial security, not by the character or spiritual integrity of their leader.

However, civic renewal does not rely only on the president. It comes from social movements committed to achieving policies which reflect national values. Today those policies will determine our national security, our public health policy, and immigration regulations that are written into law by Congress.

Immigration is one of the hot button issues that divides our citizenry. Wages for the working class in our country have not kept up with the cost of living. Many see immigration as the main cause of this abysmal wage growth. They fear that their $20.00 hour jobs can be replaced with immigrants willing to accept minimum wage. This suspicion builds resentment against them.

Joan Williams, law professor at the University of California, describes the cultural gap that informs immigration opinion. "Global elites pride themselves on their cosmopolitanism. Some younger elites reject the notion of national borders entirely. Many blue-collar whites interpret this as a shocking lack of social solidarity. They are proud to be American because it's one of the few high-status identities they can claim. Elites, on the other hand, seek social honor by presenting themselves as citizens of the world." Ms. Williams points to a 2007 study published in the *Journal of Personality and Social Psychology* which found that elites focus on achievement and individuality, while the working class prizes solidarity and loyalty, which binds them to their community.

A National Bureau of Economic Research study, led by Harvard economist Raj Chetty, reports that fewer than half of millennials born in the 1980s earn more than their parents. This wage struggle creates an unreceptive attitude toward any influx of outside cheap labor. And all of this takes place in an economy which compensates executives and CEOs at ever-increasing levels, creating a toxic division. Immigration becomes the obvious target.[11]

Most of those in the upper middle class with a college degree and secure job are sympathetic to looser immigration regulations. They classify America as a country that offers refuge to people fleeing persecution. They speak of immigrants who have come to America to get an education and have brought billions of dollars into our country. They see this diversity of population as an improvement of our society. Allowing the brightest and the best to remain has improved our American standard of living.

According to *Wall Street Journal* editorial writer, William A. Galston, most Americans do not set a high priority on a wall along the Mexican border. "They don't believe illegal immigrants are taking jobs away from native-born Americans or that they are more likely to commit crimes."[12]

Galston cites a Pew Research Center report showing that the majority of voters in both parties favor a policy that would provide a way for adults brought to this country illegally as children ("Dreamers") to remain and work and gain a way to achieve citizenship. Support among Independent voters for this policy is 80%. It represents 61% of Republicans and 69% of working class white voters. The neglect of this issue by Congress, in light of these figures, is an incredible slap in the face to most Americans. A large percentage of Americans have named immigration as one of the top three issues that Congress should deal with, ahead even of health care, the economy, jobs, and national security.

Instead of insisting that English be the only language spoken in our country, educators should encourage public schools to teach students a second or third language. The effects of bilingualism have been studied by psychologists, who have pointed out the positive correlation between bilingualism and intelligence, especially in the area of business and creativity. Psychological testing at Ohio State University, Cambridge University, and foreign academic institutions have shown the beneficial effect of bilingualism on children's cognitive development. Those advantages extend throughout the lifetime of bilingual individuals. Studies have shown that Europeans have benefited from their ability to understand multiple languages. This ability raises the intelligence quotient and delays symptoms of dementia among older adults.

Achievements in medicine, philosophy and art are influenced by the amount of openness to outside influences, and the frequency of foreign travel. Those who have not traveled far from their own neighborhood are subject to more paranoia toward the unknown — anyone who does not look or speak as they do.

I asked the CEO of an S&P 500 company — a personal friend — his opinion of the president's immigration policy.

*Nick:* "The president's policies on immigration, albeit sometimes garbed in hyperbolic rhetoric, appear to match many of the views held by everyday working people across the country. Of course, these are the segments of our population that must accommodate and absorb most of the newcomers. To the extent that immigration is temporarily dilutive, it does impact heaviest on that group. Having said that, however, it's an oversimplified and, perhaps an outright incorrect perspective to characterize those everyday people as fearing immigration. My experience is that many of those who work in factories or repair shops recognize and revere the role that immigration and the American melting pot have played in creating the society we hold so dear. Working men and women, by and large, understand the power of the American mechanism for growth: the expansion by immigration; the adoption by the newcomers of the characteristics that Americans share in common; the broad celebration of those commonalities, and the acceptance of diversity of origin and religion. Based on what you can see along the assembly lines, in the repair shops, and on the oil platforms of the United States, diversity is everywhere but the national celebration is focused on the strength that comes from the things we share in common…those characteristics that make us Americans: the beliefs… 'All men are created equal'; the patriotism…our national flag is displayed everywhere, proudly and voluntarily, and the service to our country…our veterans carry a special place in our hearts. Many of the president's supporters see his policies as efforts not to abolish or diminish this American tradition…but to make it work in the current era. For example, it's widely recognized that our nation cannot accept unlimited numbers of newcomers. Illegal immigration, therefore, must be minimized, if not by a wall, then by some other means. In a world where very many aspire to be Americans, and may have good reasons to qualify, we must have some limits and those limits imply a clear strategy for choosing who becomes an American. We've had that system in place for some time and it seemed to be efficacious. In that regard, President Trump's supporters appear to see his actions not as eliminating immigration, but as restoring that strength to its former effectiveness."

The Hoover Institution, a conservative think tank, warns that our economy desperately needs immigrants. Defense Secretary James Mattis served as a research fellow of the

Hoover Institution before being appointed by the Trump administration. Scott Minerd, a member of the Board of Overseers, has written that labor shortages are appearing in key parts of our economy, which will stifle economic growth. "US population growth has slowed, reflecting declining fertility rates and reduced net immigration inflows. The population also is aging."[13] Shortage of workers is appearing not only in highly skilled areas, but also in construction, where home builders seek drywall and framing workers. The primary constraint on the economy is the growing shortage of available workers. It will eventually result in lower living standards, according to Minerd.

"This isn't to suggest throwing open the borders," writes Minerd. "Instead, the situation requires a pragmatic, economically driven immigration approach that makes it easier for immigrants to come in legally, resolves the status of undocumented workers and Dreamers, and establishes appropriate policies and controls around future immigration."

Historically, the Dark Ages was a period of closed and protected borders. The name describes the stultifying environment which produced no cultural achievements. The Renaissance, on the other hand, which occurred in Italy and throughout Europe, produced many creative geniuses and cultural advancements in commerce and quality of life. It was associated with open borders and free trade.

Immigrants to the United States are among our most productive citizens. Foreign workers have filled positions and performed services that could not easily be filled by American workers. As the United States emerged from the great recession in 2009, this policy of selective immigration strengthened the US economy.

Franklin Delano Roosevelt once said, "We are all immigrants. We all have our own unique heritage."

Rabbi Stephen Wise was seated at a dinner next to a proud old Englishman, who told the Rabbi, "One of my ancestors signed the Declaration of Independence."

"Yes, indeed," said the rabbi. "And one of mine signed the Ten Commandments."

## Notes

1 — McCain, John with Mark Salter, *Hard Call: Great Decisions and the Extraordinary People Who Made Them,* (New York, Twelve: Hachette Book Group USA, 2007)

2 — Ibid, p. 410

3 — Ferrari, Bernard T., *Power Listening: Mastering the Most Critical Business Skill of All,* Penguin Group, New York, 2012.

4 — Pink, Daniel, *When: The Scientific Secrets of Perfect Timing,* (New York,Penguin Random House, 2018).

5 — Holmes, Jamie, *Nonsense: The Power of Not Knowing,* chapter 5, (New York, Broadway Books, 2015).

6 — JAMA, August 16, 1985, "The Accuracy of Experienced Physicians' Probability Estimates for Patients With Sore Throats," Roy M. Poses, MD; Randall D. Cebul, MD; Marjeanne Collins, MD.

7 — Noonan, Peggy, "The Left's Rage and Trump's Peril," Wall Street Journal, February 3-4, 2018

8 — Machiavelli, Niccolo (Translated by W.K. Marriott), Arc Manor, Rockville, MD., 2007.

9 — Weiss, Elaine, *"Presidential Hush Money, Circa 1920,"* Wall Street Journal, Saturday/Sunday, June 2-3, 2018. Ms. Weiss's latest book, "The Woman's Hour: The Great Fight to Win the Vote," was published in March by Viking.

10 — Ibid.

11 — Williams, Joan C., "The Elites Feed Anti-Immigrant Bias," article in the Wall Street Journal, Tuesday, July 10, 2018. Ms. Williams is a law professor at the University of California, Hastings, and author of "White Working Class" (Harvard Business Review, 2017).

12 — Galston, William A., "Americans Want an Immigration Deal," Wall Street Journal section "Politics & Ideas, Wednesday, July 11, 2018.

13 — Minerd, Scott, "Our Economy Needs Immigrants, Desperately," editorial published in *Barron's* magazine, July 30, 2018.

# Chapter 17

# Rules For Survival

*There are only two things a child will share willingly
— communicable diseases and his mother's age.*
Dr. Benjamin Spock, US pediatrician and
psychiatrist

Before going to bed last night I examined the pictures
on Facebook of the children my daughter Laura is teaching.
My daughter posts these for parents, families, and friends
so that they can observe the children's educational progress
in the classroom. Each picture shows a child reading a book
or smiling at the camera. Parents love these pictures. They
post their own, showing their child at bedtime absorbed in
a book or reading a story to a puzzled looking baby brother.
I click the "like" word on each picture and comment on a
few of them.

These images must have restored my own childhood
memories. I dreamed about them last night. I was five years
old and beginning to become aware of the existence and
importance of words. I remember seeing the word "look"
written by my first grade teacher on the blackboard. What a
strange word, with two eyes poking out of the middle. How
queer it appeared to me. And in the evening I marveled as I
watched my father reading the newspaper, wondering how
he could make any sense out of that mess of black marks on
a huge page. He must be a genius, I thought to myself.

Then a vision of my mother came back. It was evening.
I was three and my sister, Julie, was six. Mother was sitting
on the top step of the stairway of our little house in Ash-
land, Ohio, reading a book chapter as she did each night before we fell asleep. The book was about a cat. The title was

*When in Doubt, Lick.* We used to laugh about that title and give that advice to each other when confused. My mother and father snickered about it, and I realize now that they were probably giving it other meanings. Their love for each other was volatile, but at times very evident in its physicality. Those were good memories.

But there were times when I went to school feeling defeated and afraid. It was when my parents had argued. It made me feel unloved and insecure. I carried the stress throughout the day and feared what I might find when I returned home: loving conversation or coldness and criticism.

My mother had a volatile temper which erupted quickly when she was angry with me. When I was seventeen years old, she objected to the girl I was dating. She demanded that I must stop seeing this girl. Her criticism turned into a shouting match between us, during which she shouted at me: "Get out!"

So I did. For three days I hid at the girlfriend's house. When the local police came looking for me, I hid in the closet under a pile of umbrellas, clothes, and shoes. I left the next day for Dallas, Texas.

*We begin to live when we conceive life as a tragedy.*
W.B. Yeats, *Autobiography*

With $20 in the pocket of my jeans, I booked a room at a boarding house for $2 a night, including breakfast. I worked a small construction job, but got laid off after two days because I knew nothing about carpentry tools. I read an advertisement in the newspaper for a manual labor job at a small business. I interviewed for the janitorial job, but was not hired because the business owner was not satisfied with my answer to his question, "What is personality?" A dumb question anyway, I thought to myself. The job was sweeping and cleaning restrooms. "It's all about attitude, kid. Yes, that's right, attitude. We like to see intelligent smiles on our faces around here." I asked him how he defined personality.

He said, "It's the ability to smile while you're cleaning the toilet bowl." I think he made that up.

I was hungry and found a Salvation Army where I could get a free warmed-up meal if I listened to the 45-minute fire-and-brimstone sermon from the Major. I was also given another shirt to replace the ragged one I was wearing.

At the Salvation Army I met a 6'7" black ex-convict who played guitar — rhythm and blues. Since we had nothing in common, we took a strange, curious liking to each other. He invited me to join his band and add a Satchmo, Dixieland trumpet touch to their repertoire.

The bar was off a side street in a Dallas slum. It was a smoke-filled, cracker box sized room. But when the music poured off the small elevated stage and reverberated around the walls, every young girl and guy in the room was bumping and grinding on the dance floor.

During the breaks, I melted in with the band members out in the alley behind the bar. My musician companions smoked pot. They danced by themselves and sang blues melodies in harmony that echoed off the walls of the buildings enclosing the alley. Coming from a segregated country village, I sat and watched in awe and curiosity.

One night when I returned home from a gig at three o'clock in the morning, a girl and her mother who were temporarily staying at the same boarding house, were waiting up for me. The girl was no more than fifteen and her mother not much over thirty. They told me they were going to New Orleans the next day. They offered convincing reasons why I should go with them. They made it evident that they were both available to me. But even more enticing was the thought of playing in the New Orleans blues bands. I had grown up listening to Gatemouth broadcast from the Roosevelt Hotel. Back home I had a stack of Blues and Dixieland records that had worn out half a dozen needles on my record player. It was a tempting offer, and accepting it would have resulted in a different life than the one I am now living. The hand of providence must have intervened. I turned down the offer. A few weeks later my parents discovered where I was and made arrangements for my return home. From there I was sent to another state for redemption.

From birth we possess a psychological propensity for self-preservation — both physical and emotional — a survival instinct. Our first act is to scream for nourishment. As we mature we learn to temper the scream, to negotiate for our needs. When raised in a healthy environment, disciplined comportment displaces angry demands. To the degree that discipline is lacking, self-indulgence becomes the approach to daily life. I want what I want, because I deserve it. My needs are more important than yours. The satisfaction of my desires is essential even if it impedes your happiness.

Spiritual discipline enlarges the scope of our world view. It balances the self-directed focus of the ego. It inspires an outward reach beyond self-interest. In its best manifestations, religion inspires compassion, self-sacrifice. A contrite faith is the acknowledgement that we may have not only a limited knowledge of physical reality, but an even more meager awareness of the metaphysical realm.

Religious practice — worship, prayer, scripture study — when conducted in a healthy-minded environment, can enhance human compatibility. It provides measurable benefits to communities at large as well as marriages and family relationships.

The Code of Hammurabi, which pre-dated the recording of the Ten Commandments, originated in order to provide the rules for sustainable communal living. Survival of community demanded concern beyond self-interest. It required respect for the lives and possessions of others. So important was this to the survival of the human race that the first commandment of Moses was a requirement to revere the Source of these dictums, who became known in the Judeo-Christian tradition as Yahweh, God. This creator was to be so venerated that his name was only to be spoken in respect. Only by recognizing the supreme power of this creator would humanity be able to envision life outside their own solipsistic perception of reality.

The earliest moral requirement of the Judeo-Christian message was simple. But it became lost in an accretion of definitions. Embedded in doctrinal detail, it required chosen officials to interpret its meaning and guard against defilement of the message which had become attached to dozens of rules. Conflicting interpretations began to evolve; their adherents divided into factions and denominations, embroiled in unrestrained conflict. Vindictive judgment displaced the original message.

What was the singular message from which these battling tribes emerged? Two rules: first, hold in greatest esteem the source of life. Second, treat every human being with unqualified acceptance.

The story goes that an expert in the law posed a question. It might have been something like this:

"Teacher, you put yourself out there as a legal expert. So what is the greatest commandment in the law?"

"Well, it's simple. It goes back to the earliest recorded law (Leviticus 19:17-18). Don't seek revenge or bear a grudge against anyone; but love your neighbor as much as you love yourself."

"Love my neighbor? You must not know *my* neighbor. Sure! You say it's simple, but simple can mean boneheaded."

"Don't try to obfuscate. The 'simple' I'm talking about means pure, sincere, and uncomplicated. First you tangle it in detail. Then you ignore it. You bring clerics on board to preach it, moralists to define it, directors to manage it."

✠ ✠ ✠

We are far removed from that ancient message which simply commanded tolerance and forgiveness. Simplicity is boring and unsustainable. We venerate complexity. We become mired in the detail. "Our life is frittered away by detail," wrote Henry David Thoreau. "Simplify, simplify."

Federal laws are contained in more than 50,000 volumes of over 223,000 pages. There are 20,000 laws just governing the use and ownership of guns. It all started with ten ancient laws which became Ten Commandments. They are plainly applied, for example, in marriage vows, "to love and to cherish, 'til death us do part." Weekly messages command that the silent listeners refrain from holding grudges. Children sing, "Red and yellow, black and white, they are equal in His sight."

And every day, everywhere a common response is heard, "Yes....but...!"

# Chapter 18

# What Is Piety?

*He prayeth best, who loveth best*
*All things both great and small;*
*For the dear God who loveth us,*
*He made and loveth all.*
    Samuel Taylor Coleridge

Looking back over my nearly four-score years, I recall moments in my life that were of consequence: when I sat for an hour in the small kitchen with 99-year-old Willa, listening to her share the story of her life and faith: a husband who had died sixty years ago when she was 39 years old, leaving her to raise five children, one of whom died in a farm accident; when I stood by a crib in a Haitian orphanage, trying to comfort a three-month-old baby abandoned at birth by a mother who already had too many babies to feed; when I held my temper and tried to listen patiently to a man for whom I felt only revulsion. Maybe those were moments of sanctity, reverence. What else does it mean?

Willa would say it means, "Little children, love one another." Can I choose which people I love? Apparently I can not. That Jewish carpenter taught that one must accept with compassion each person: the nasty neighbor, the difficult boss, those noisy teenagers, and anyone else, whether they look and act like me or not. No wonder biblical morality is ignored.

✚ ✚ ✚

During my morning run a song continued to loop continuously through my mind: "There's a wideness in God's mercy, like the wideness of the sea…", instead of the painful reflection of what I had just read in the morning paper: the forty-year sentence handed down to a fifteen-year-old girl who three years before had lured a classmate into the woods and brutally stabbed her multiple times, leaving her for dead; the failure of Michigan State officials to respond to reliable reports of sex abuse of young female Olympic athletes by the team's doctor; the rampant spread of flu overwhelming hospital staff. By the time you read this it will all be old news, replaced by other tragic events, the reporting of which drives newspaper sales. Somehow I had buried all this under the words: "There's wideness in God's mercy… there is no place where earth's sorrows are more felt than up in heaven…"

Many years of participation in worship services planted these words, which have continued to loop through my memory. They give a context to my life. They bring modest comfort. I'm grateful for learning the message. But now I view it from a different perspective; like the size of the apple trees in my back yard, which seemed less ascendant and daunting when I became older. I leave room for doubt and questions.

At my age what seems most essential about worship is what is simple: unmediated and unadorned. Maybe the ornate stained glass windows and symphonic choirs elevate human accomplishment as much as spiritual reflection. The priestly robes, the burning candles, the pulpit oratory might not be as likely to remind me of a mysterious "ground of being." They seem to be more representative of the accouterments of a man-made institution.[1] I am entertained by the angelic voices of the choir, but, as I listen, I might be more inclined to praise the choir members than to praise God. When the preacher enters his pulpit and starts to deliver an inspiring message, I am more likely to think 'what a great preacher,' rather than 'what a great God.'

In the church where I grew up, the choir never directly faced the congregation, but directed their singing toward the altar when presenting an anthem. This arrangement made evident the fact that this was not entertainment for the enjoyment of the congregation, but an offering to the almighty. The same was true of a soloist, who always faced at an angle between the altar and the congregation. The intention and purpose of worship became firmly entrenched the first time I was given the answer to the question I asked as a child, "Why doesn't that man look at us when he sings a solo?" It created an effective and long lasting memory in my mind. I have never since seen a choir anthem or solo presented in this way.

Will a time ever come when churches, temples, synagogues, and mosques focus on the spiritual rather than the physical; a place where the emphasis is on our potential, not our performance? It might be a community that provides an environment of openness and discourse, where people gather to find the common ground of their humanity; where acceptance of others does not imply that their political or philosophical views have to meet with the tacit approval of everyone else. When places of worship are welcoming to those of different political persuasion and diverse religious perceptions, they will become the communities where civil discourse is discovered, an oasis from the raging accusations and hate-filled discourse of pundits and self-aggrandizing bullies. Otherwise churches are no different from the civil societies which organize according to a secular mission statement or a political philosophy.

Those who base their faith on a specific religious platform are wise to acknowledge with humility that where dogma has trumped compassion, the church has been responsible for suffering. We witness too many people with strong religious affiliations uttering caustic, judgmental comments about their neighbors or those of a different ethnicity. Beware of those folks whose self-proclaimed piety overrides their compassion.

It would be refreshing to find a religious community where non-judgment was a priority, where hospitality was extended, where strangers of widely diverse opinions could enter and become friends. From the Christian perspective, this represents the simply stated great commandment to "love God…and love our neighbor as ourselves." Loving our fellow human beings does not require a particular religious affiliation. The challenge is to create that type of community where folks with a wide range of viewpoints and beliefs can join together not as rivals seeking to do battle, but as fellow strugglers who are seeking the truth through openness and questions. This may be a utopian ideal. While we may not be able to achieve it, we can be transformed in our attempt to reach for it.

I continue to hold fast to my skeptical faith, and I reserve the right to ask questions, to continue seeking the truth.

*Where non-judgment was a priority…*

Most relationships, in order to endure, learn to tolerate minor irritating behavior. He accepts the way she squeezes the toothpaste in the middle; she doesn't say anything about the sloppy way he loads the dishwasher. The spoiled child in us says, 'I don't have to tolerate that way of doing it.' We tell ourselves that it is 'constructive' criticism to point out certain behavior. We soon learn that there is no such thing as 'constructive' criticism. All criticism elicits a self-defensive response. To think it is our duty to correct the behavior of others turns us into carping cynics. It's what leads partners to distance themselves from each other. Fear of criticism will soon destroy a healthy relationship.

In a marriage enrichment seminar I conducted, many women admitted that it was negative judgment from their husbands that had destroyed their interest in a sexual relationship.

Accepting criticism without discussion indicates an unhealthy personality or a sick relationship. A woman may fear to defend herself in order to avoid her partner's rage. A man who submits with no self-defense indicates a neurotic need to avoid conflict. We don't change that easily. And a healthy-minded person does not submit to the crushing judgment of others. Likewise we resist setting ourselves up as judges of other's conduct if we want a partner to continue enjoying our presence.

Early in a courtship the man is full of praise and compliments. The woman appreciates this attention. It makes her feel good about herself when she is with him. They marry. After several months he notices that she talks too much. And she realizes that he doesn't change his shirt every day, doesn't take a shower often enough. Negative comments intrude. Judgments are made. "I'm just being honest with you," she says. How many married couples destroy one another by "being honest." Soon it becomes ridicule. It creates a slow bleeding of affection. Being with her no longer makes him feel good about himself the way it did at first. And she no longer has any desire to please him after listening to his complaints. Each one is incapable of restraint. The need to criticize, to render judgment, has become more important than maintaining harmony in the marriage. Criticism has a destructive power which can creep into a relationship and cause each partner to retreat into a silent self-defense.

One can find the same spirit of judgment in some religious communities. At first we feel welcome: 'come as you are,' is the invitation. But after the initiation period, the welcome spirit becomes tainted with the realization that these folks inside the community of faith are no different from those outside: they gossip, they show intolerance for ethnic differences. They say the right words, but their actions speak more loudly.

Skepticism can engender self-reflection, even self-judgment, which is more easily accepted than judgment from others. We step back and look at ourselves as others see us, as our partner sees us, and we ask, 'Do I like this person I've become?'

✚ ✚ ✚

Over half a century ago I married the youngest daughter of my ethics professor. It is a wonder that the marriage ever came to pass because I gave the man every reason to dislike me, and withhold his permission for me to marry his daughter. I caught sight of her when she was still in high school, a number of years younger than me. I thought she looked remarkably like the Swedish actress Bridget Bardot. She refused my first advances, but after several attempts she accepted an invitation to a movie — *The Cardinal.* We discovered a mutual attraction — intellectually and physically. She was highly intelligent, had a cheery disposition, and laughed at my jokes. After several dates she accepted my ridiculously impulsive suggestion to elope. We left Ohio late at night and drove to a resort location where we intended to carry out our scheme. After just two days it became evident that the plan would have to be abandoned. She was too young to marry without parental consent. Having come to my senses, I returned her to her front door, red-faced and embarrassed, without going into the house to attempt an explanation. But I still had to face Dr. Kantonen, her father, a month later as my ethics professor. Would he condemn me? Would he flunk me?

I was astonished the first time I saw him after the kidnapping of his daughter and he greeted me warmly without referring to that shameful past. That was when I discovered that he lived by the grace-laden gospel he proclaimed. He was not one to hold grudges.

The past never held as much interest for him as the future with its creative possibilities. On his eightieth birthday he was talking about his ninetieth, rather than the past eighty years. And on his ninetieth birthday he declared what he intended to be doing on his hundredth. In the same month that he died, he discussed with his wife their plan to drive to Boston again to see his beloved Red Sox play. That was his nature: to look forward, plan ahead, not dwell on the past.

His memorial service was a victory celebration. Voices rose in singing, scriptures recalled the promises of God; the pastor's message expressed the blessings that his life had bestowed upon everyone. As a leading theologian and professor he had influenced thousands of students. His books had been translated into dozens of languages. He had lectured at theology schools, universities, and educational conferences in various parts of the United States, Canada, and Europe. And yet he had requested that no one look backward over his life. That wasn't his style. He always looked to the future. And I'm sure that's why he chose the hymn that was sung before his body was laid to rest:

Hold thou the cross before my closing eyes.
Shine through the gloom, and point me to the skies;
Heav'n's morning breaks, and earth's vain shadows flee;
In life, in death, O Lord, abide with me.

## Notes

1 — Beware of the teachers of the law. They like to walk around in flowing robes and love to be greeted with respect in the marketplaces and have the most important seats in the synagogues and the places of honor at banquets (Luke 20:45).

# Chapter 19

# Generations

*The generation of living things pass in a short time,*
*and like runners hand on the torch of life.*
   Lucretius, "On the Nature of Things"

The telephone call came to my office. It was 10:25 a.m. on a cold and wintry day in early December. My mother: "We're downtown behind the bank. Dad has fallen on the ice and needs to go to the hospital. You need to come over right away. He is really hurt." I had two salesmen waiting to see me. A truck had pulled up to the warehouse and was waiting to be unloaded (my warehouse men were out on a delivery.) The sales floor had just notified me that a customer wanted to talk to me about purchasing a $10,000 office suite.

This accumulation of demands was a typical scenario for a private business owner with non-existent layers of management available to take over in situations such as these. But the urgent phone call was the kind of message that sounds like "your house is on fire, you'd better do something now." So I ran out the back door to my van and hurried to where they were waiting.

When I drove into the bank parking lot I could see through his stoic facade the pain in dad's face, even though he stood properly erect as if at attention. As was his custom, he was dressed in suit and tie, a long overcoat and the signature fedora hat, always considered in his day the *de rigueur* for men going out in public.

After pulling up to the back door of the bank I struggled to load him into the van. As soon as he was seated, he slumped over and burst into tears, immediately apologizing for being such a "sissy." We drove four blocks to the hospital and signed him in for examination. After sitting for an exasperating 45 minutes in the emergency waiting room, he was admitted, x-rayed and told that he had five broken ribs. In retrospect I realize that these experiences were similar to those described by Sherwin Nuland in his book *How We Die,* in which he described the gradual deterioration of his aging grandmother who lived with him. What I was witnessing was the early stages of my father's decline: the loss of physical agility at the age of 71.

My father was an academically oriented Lutheran minister and college president with a Yale Ph.D. Mother was a fundamentalist Baptist with a college degree in home economics. Their personalities were as complimentary as pancakes and potato salad. The disparity created stress, but it was never boring. The range of emotions in their more than sixty-year marriage was inclusive of affection, rage, jealousy, devotion. Dissension was unpredictable, but always resolved at the end of the day with the required routine of family devotions, which cleared the air of any stormy atmosphere. Those half-hour devotional periods were concluded only after what seemed like an interminable Baptist prayer. It was not always clear as to whether the emotional supplication was being directed toward the Almighty or the other family members around the kitchen table. When we were being alerted to the appointed hour for family devotions, my sister would whisper to me, "time for emotions." Compulsory spiritual exercises included a prayer before every meal, as well as a bedtime prayer by my father after we were tucked in.

After her death at age 91, my father was grief-stricken for many weeks. Underlying that range of emotional interaction was admiration and respect.

*A marriage can withstand strong emotions — anger and jealousy. It can survive almost everything except contempt. In past years when I discussed marriage plans with a couple, I asked them to answer several questions about their partner, such as what would you change about him/her? During that discussion I looked for signs of disdain or impatience. If many of the responses were made with a rolling of the eyes, sarcasm, or especially a sign of contempt, it was a sign of an ultimately doomed marriage. Arrogance and dismissiveness were an indication that the man or woman was not prepared to make sacrifices while living under the same roof with a spouse.*

There were several disadvantages to living in the same town with aging parents: the sense that I was under the critical surveillance of observers belonging to another generation; the obligation to make frequent visits, which at times were not only inopportune but boring; the responsibility of preparing them for my absence whenever I was traveling out of town on business. The advantage of this proximity, however, was the preview it presented to me of my own future decline and demise, and how it could affect my children.

While my parents' lives had been marked by outstanding achievements, which were reflected in the beauty of their home and surroundings, these became meaningless and were stripped away layer by layer as they grew older. Through various transitions and physical moves they went from a college president's home on the shores of Lake Michigan, to a typical middle class neighborhood residence, to a condominium apartment, to independent living in a nursing home; and finally to the assisted living wing with a bed in a shared room and a few possessions that could be entirely contained in a small dresser, a nightstand and a shared closet.

I observed how the significance of possessions diminished in my parents' lives as they aged. They provided little comfort or support in their preparation for their last years. I realize that as I age *things* will appropriately lose their priority in my life. The spaciousness of my house, the size of my bank account, the extent of my wardrobe, all of these will begin to lose their ability to satisfy my soul's longing for something that has more significant meaning.

Although my father had accomplished commendable achievements during his lifetime, I observed how little his ambition served him as his body withered and he became more dependent upon the assistance of his "skilled care" helpers for even the basic functions of eating and even defecating.

The half dozen books he had written and published were among the few items important enough to be left out for display on the nightstand by his bed. But they were little noticed or discussed by any of the aides or employees who came in to assist him. While his authoritarian manner and respected position had always prompted people to address him as "Dr. Lentz," he was now unceremoniously called just Harold, or "Honey." As he drifted into the dotage of his early 90s this intimacy seemed to appeal at times to his lonely heart. During his earlier years at the nursing home the overly familiar greeting had grated on his proper nature. Throughout his life as a pastor and college president he had been addressed with dignity and respect. All that changes when you are reduced to being a victim of the night nurse who enters before bedtime to insert a catheter.

Two of his possessions were mentioned during the eulogy delivered by Carthage College President Gregory Campbell: the Bible on his nightstand and the small, embroidered sign "Jesus" on his dresser. These said nothing about what he had accomplished or what he had acquired in his 93 years. Rather they signified the inward qualities of his spirit. As I reflected on these changes in his life I came to understand more fully the utter insignificance of the accomplishments we consider to be so important in our lives. Life is a matter of "climbing down 10,000 ladders until we shake hands with the little clod of earth that we are" as Karl Jung once put it.

It was his deeply ingrained spiritual qualities which came to his aid as he lay dying. On one of my last visits I entered his room where he was sleeping and found him clutching his Bible to his chest. It was as though the message in this book gave him something tangible to grasp for assurance; something in which he could find comfort from the disquietude of death; it represented assurance of love and acceptance. During the last months he did not speak about matters of faith and religion, but when I asked him to pray following the reading of devotions, his prayer was articulate, fervent and fluent, reflecting the openness of communion with his God.

Growing up in this home environment cultivated the ground for questions and skepticism. But now, years later, in moments of desolation, I hear myself mentally repeating biblical verses that I learned when I was ten-years-old: *the Lord is my shepherd... oh give thanks to the Lord, for he is good... the Lord loves a cheerful giver.* At times I discover that I have been humming a gospel hymn that I learned from Wednesday night prayer meetings when I was eight-years-old: *What a Friend We Have in Jesus; Amazing Grace; He Leadeth Me.* The words of these songs reside somewhere among the layers of memory and emerge at unexpected moments when my musings may be far from pious reflection. Although I was impatient at times, I am grateful now that I was able to observe their decline and death. It helped me learn more about myself and what is important as I grow older:

I find that spiritual growth is difficult, but becomes more important as we grow older. I am referring to things of the spirit, not religious observance. I am learning that patient listening is more important than winning an argument. Silence is often the best answer. My daily activity quickly becomes filled with "to do" lists of things that are ultimately meaningless. They distract from the challenge of looking inward, fearful of what might be missing. Although no one talks about it in normal daily conversation, spiritual growth will become more important than getting everything done on the list. I will spend more time in contemplation of "core values" and — through meditation — a deepening communion with my inner self and how "I" relate to life's depth.

"Letting go" will be more useful to me as I grow older. That means releasing my grip on anything I consider to be my own—possessions, honors, relationships. Relinquishing my desires to the ebb and flow and circumstance of life will soften my character, open my mind and accommodate my spirit as I age and decline. This doesn't happen overnight, but I notice the subduing of my irritability, my willingness to let aggravating statements go by without comment. (The growth of this process, however, is often interrupted by irrational moments of sensitivity, accompanied by flashes of my old anger.)

Allow others to be as they are: don't attempt to change their behavior. It only leads to disappointment and frustration. This especially applies to my children, close friends and associates. I must learn to respect their individuality and to accept that their views are often different from my own.

Develop stillness and the ability to flow with events as they happen. Practice focusing on the satisfaction of "being alive." Stop resisting the circumstances over which I have no control. Be receptive and open to circumstances.

There will come a time when I will no longer have control over even the most basic functions of my life. Learn with humility that my desire for self-sufficiency can only lead to sterile isolation.

Teach less, listen more. I noticed, with surprise, that my father, who I had thought always had all the answers, began to question *me* about not only worldly matters, but also about the circumstances of his own life. Life is full of unknowns, the greatest of which is death. Looking at life as being full of unknowns will help me become more open and receptive, less rigid about my own opinions. I will ask more questions and introspectively challenge my own convictions.

My daily priorities should be focused, in descending order on:

*Being and becoming*: kindness, patience, tolerance; concentration on core values, tempered by curiosity and acceptance.

*Doing*: activities that satisfy the personal need for learning, physical development, social life with others, helpfulness — volunteerism, service to others.

*Having*: simplify; determine what is essential and what is superfluous; discipline the desire for acquisition and possessions; eliminate "entertainment" shopping in lieu of creative activity.

✚ ✚ ✚

It has been said that consumerism is an unofficial, corporate-sponsored world religion, whose evangelism is advertisement, whose church is the mall, and whose values are appearance and affluence. It is a religion without character, without promise, and without hope.

During the last three years of their lives, I went to the convalescent home every Friday. I would eat dinner with my father, who remained mentally sharp to the end of his days. Then I went to sit and hold hands for an hour with my mother, whose mind was adrift, but whose spirit was always pleasant. The lessons I learned from those visits were unspoken, but obvious. Nothing they had acquired throughout their lifetime retained the least significance; no treasures that had held so many memories served them, comforted them, or sustained them.

Now in my seventh decade of life, it is easier to break the grip of acquisition. I wish it had happened sooner. From the Desert Fathers has come eternal wisdom: "The desire for possessions is dangerous and terrible, knowing no satiety; it drives the soul which it controls to the heights of evil."

We live in a time of material affluence and spiritual poverty. We place great value on things that can be seen, touched, possessed. We have put away as childish what some call the superstitions and mysticism which guided previous generations. But that renunciation has left a void. The emptiness of spiritual abandonment does not breed contentment. For many, life is a matter of filling time with unreflective busyness, shopping, dining, and acquiring in order to escape the hours of boredom interrupted by intermittent moments of panic. I remember hearing the message in church decades ago: Unless you break your attachment to your possessions — your things — you will not be able to nurture the inner character for which you were created (Matthew 19: 20f).

When something upset my high school daughter, her boyfriend would tell her, "It ain't nothin' but a thing." He may have been wise beyond his years. *Things* don't last; they aren't important, so what has happened to you is no more important than a thing.

> *At the end of the game, the king and the pawn go back into the same box.*
> Italian proverb

# Chapter 20

# Varieties Of Worship: From Snakes To Strychnine

*The best religion is the most tolerant.*
Mme.de Girardin, d. 1855

From the beginning of human history, religious rituals have been invented in an attempt either to extend life or to experience a spiritual connection. A variety of religious precepts and observances exist in our country and around the world.

Jehovah Witnesses refuse blood transfusions based on various biblical scriptures (Genesis 9:4; Leviticus 17:10, Acts 15:28,29).

The Digambara, one of the two sects of Jainism, wear no clothes. They don't consider themselves to be naked, because they claim that they are wearing the environment. (Note to frustrated exhibitionists: the city fathers are unlikely to accept the explanation that you are a Digambara convert.)

The Jewish ritual of *Kaparot* consists of grasping a live chicken by the wings and moving it around one's head three times. It is a symbolic transfer of sins to the chicken. (Don't try this in public.)

Members of the Yanomami tribe who live in the Amazon rainforest of Brazil eat the burned ashes and bones of their dead after mixing them with food such as bananas. This keeps the spirit of the individual alive.

Some denominations of the Latter Day Saints wear sacred under garments. The clothing is worn by those adults who have participated in ritual ceremony known as a washing and anointing ordinance.

At the southern tip of West Virginia lies a tiny crossroads village named Jolo. It is situated among other small mountain villages with names like Panther, War, Yukon, Mohawk, and Excelsior. If you ride a few miles out of town from Jolo, and take a side road into the woods you will come across a white frame building. There's no sign out front, but a small cross on the entrance door indicates it might be a church of some kind.

In 1994, I read a newspaper article about a church in West Virginia where the worship services included handling poisonous vipers and drinking strychnine. I was fascinated and curious. My wife suggested it would make a nice camping trip on the Harley. I agreed. But she said it would have to be a solo trip.

A camping trip on a Harley requires careful planning if it's going to include a tent, sleeping bag, towel, flashlight, and a change of clothing. In order to scale down and simplify even a camera — in that day before cell phones — seemed like unnecessary baggage. Memories and journal notes would have to do.

I drove out of Lima, Ohio, on a sunny June afternoon, baffle-free Harley mufflers rumbling greedily, and soon was singing at the top of my lungs as I rode south on route 117. The roar of the engine drowned me out, but a few farmers looked up in bemusement. By late afternoon I had arrived at Delphi on the edge of the Wayne National Forest for my first night of camping at Tar Hollow State Park. I picked an idyllic spot near a stream to set up camp.

I slept soundly and awoke to blue skies and sunshine. After a breakfast of protein bar washed down with pump water, I set out and rode another 251 miles to Chief Logan State Park in West Virginia, where I discovered the perfect location: a solitary camp site on top of a mountain knoll. During the evening a deer grazed within twenty feet of my camp site, as I sat quietly meditating and reading sections of Andrew Weil's book *Spontaneous Healing*. The next morning I discovered that my maps and AAA camp books had been removed from the saddle bags of the motorcycle by raccoons. They had made a dinner out of several pages of the book and corners of the maps. But they were all salvageable.

I stopped in Rossmore (population 301) at Ettie's Restaurant for lunch and ordered black beans and cornbread for $1.47. Ettie served me enough to fill up for the rest of the day. But after a hard afternoon ride I was hungry again and stopped in southern West Virginia at the curiously named "Hemlock Restaurant." The lone waitress/cook could not explain the reason for the morbid name, nor did she seem to understand the lethal connotation.

Appalachia breeds a different mentality in its inhabitants. Life spans are shorter, life is harder, domestic abuse and violence is more common. A sign by the side of the road in a junk-filled yard read *No Trespassing. Survivors Will Be Prosecuted.* I could imagine the owner of the dilapidated property sitting inside with a shotgun.

When it came time to find the location of the snake-handling church, it proved more difficult than I had anticipated. In Jolo I stopped at a small, old-fashioned, corner gas station/convenience store and chatted with several local girls who were hanging around the front. One girl's outfit barely covered her assets. She may have seen more ceilings than Michelangelo. The others could be described variously as load bearing hips, big-boned, especially in the knuckles.

"What do you do for excitement here in Jolo, West Virginia," I asked?

"Folks in Jolo don't get excited," was the slow, drawn out drawl of an answer. Pushing it a little further I was finally informed that the usual weekend entertainment was to "drive up the mountain on Friday night, drink beer, and shoot coon."

After riding up and down the mountain roads that evening, I finally found *The Church of the Lord Jesus.* Turns out I had passed it several times without knowing it, because there was no marker by the road indicating that it was a church.

Inside, the service had already started. But it was unlike any church service I had ever attended before. I had feared that, as an outsider, I might not be accepted, but my entrance didn't cause any undue attention. Maybe it was the dust and dirt-covered jeans and T-shirt, and the well-worn leather coat that made my presence appear that I was entitled to be there as much as anyone else.

I looked around. A gaunt-faced woman bent over a keyboard, pouring out a gospel blues hymn with deep-felt emotion. She looked ancient; like she'd been around since before the Dead Sea got sick. Drums, bass, and guitar made up the rest of the ensemble. Thin, reedy voices wailed the lyrics of pain, sorrow and salvation. Most of the musicians had the look of under-fed concentration camp survivors.

As the hour progressed the music took on a more compelling beat. The children became more restless and wandered in and out of the church pews, running up and down the aisles. Finally the music faded, a stillness fell over the small gathering and Brother Bob Elkins laid down his guitar and stood up to preach.

For the next hour he harangued the congregation about the evil that would befall those who neglected to come to church. As he talked, I looked around at the strange crowd. I noticed the three boxes with Plexiglas lids on the front step of the chancel area, in front of the altar. That had to be where the snakes were, I thought.

Finally Brother Elkins extended the invitation for any who needed spiritual healing and the laying-on-of-hands to come forward to receive divine blessing. I was ready to stretch my legs, but more importantly, I was curious about the contents of the three boxes with the Plexiglas lids. So along with four or five others, I stepped forward to receive the prayers of consecration.

Meanwhile the music took on a more urgent, hypnotic beat and folks began dancing in the aisles, some in a clogging-style two step, and others in a rhythmic stomping from one side to the other. I felt the preacher's hand on my head and listened to his fervent prayer for my spiritual healing. Other worshipers surrounded me placing their arms on my back and around my waist. The combination of the throbbing music and the chanting prayer spoken over my head started to send me into a trance-like state of euphoria…until I noticed one of the men lean down and remove the padlocks from the three boxes. His arm was swollen and covered with lesions, which he had been scratching incessantly during the prayer session. Snake venom from forty-three bites, I later learned. Writhing vipers began to make their escape from the boxes. An obese man walked to the altar, picked up a mason jar and swallowed a small amount.

As I furtively looked about for an escape route, several men and women began picking up the snakes and wrapping them around their arms and necks, gently stroking the undersides of each serpent. Penned in by snakes and people, I decided it would be too cowardly to jump over the front pew and trample the women and children in the front rows. My only option was to stand still and not volunteer exposing my unwilling flesh to the viperous fangs.

At the first opportunity I made my exit and stood outside to calm my nerves as the service was drawing to a close. When my eyes adjusted to the darkness I noticed another member of the congregation leaning against his pickup, smoking a cigarette. I ambled over and took advantage of his willingness to talk by asking him about the meaning of what I had just witnessed. The passage from the gospel of Mark 16:18 was unknown to him: *They will pick up snakes with their hands; and when they drink deadly poison, it will not hurt them at all.*

"I come here because it's the best Saturday night entertainment around these mountains," he informed me. "And it's a lot cheaper than going to the clubs and drinking. Besides I think the preacher is real sincere."

When I walked back inside the church I was relieved to see that the knot of hissing, writhing copperheads and rattlers had been re-ensconced in their shelter. The service ended happily as no one on this particular Saturday night had been inflicted with a snake bite. Other times the outcome had not been so fortunate. One member of the church has a maimed left hand from 86 snakebites. Another man, a musician in the church band, had lost his wife a few months earlier from a snake bite. I learned later that a national broadcasting company had visited the church a year before. They took a sample of the liquid displayed in the Mason jar on the altar and sent it to an independent lab for analysis. It proved to be mildly diluted strychnine.

What drives this frantic search for authenticity of religious experience? Immune to pain from years of suffering, they take extreme measures to reach heightened emotionality. Life is cheap; there is little joy. Could it be that in order to revive deadened feelings, which have been destroyed by deprivation, abuse, and lack of warmth or affection, they pursue an authentic religious experience through death defying spiritual practice? Maybe they prove faith to themselves and others by tempting death.

Outside the church again after the service had ended several young boys, ten to twelve years old, stood around admiring my red Harley. Each one wanted to take a turn sitting on it. One told me, "When ya'll come back, I'll ride on that motorcycle with you 'cause I have a leather coat."

As any Harley rider will tell you, "It's not the destination, it's the journey," and on this particular journey I was enriched by the conversations with those I met along the way. There were Jackie and Becky, two elderly ladies who invited me to sit by their campfire, drink coffee, and share stories. They camp out together several weeks each summer to escape the boredom of their husbands who are content to sit on the porch and drink beer all day. And there was the grizzled, ex-marine in the camp ground who is now a professional mural painter and story teller. He entertains campers with tales of civil war battles, describing how families were split when they took sides between the north and the south. "Always do something that will outlast you," he said, quoting Will James, one of his favorite philosophers.

As fascinating as each of these encounters were, it is the memory of that Saturday night service at The Church of the Lord Jesus that continues to haunt me in the midnight hour of my sleepless moments. The diversity of human nature is almost as unfathomable as is the mind of a creator. And while we might find a unity in our desire to comprehend his nature, we will no doubt never entirely agree on how to interpret his word or approach his presence.

Chapter 21

# The Final Breath...

TJ*: I wonder if he can still hear us since he's had the stroke.

Laura: Ask him to squeeze your hand if he knows what you are saying.

Okay.

TJ: Yes! He did. He must be hearing us.

A small hand on my neck, Selby, the physician's assistant: he still has a weak pulse.

The whispers of my children, my grandchildren and my wife circle above my bed. They're all here; the most important people in my life. Mental images of each one flash through my mind.

What have four score odd years produced? What am I leaving behind? After they're done dividing up the accounts, what will they say about my life?

> Tuula...well...he once told me....
> Eeva ...he sure was....
> Marty...did  I ever tell you about the time he....

There's no more pain...insensate drifting. Images from the past...walking up the road on summer evenings to watch the sunset over Indian Lake. "If you've seen one, you've seen them all," a neighbor, Tim, yells once again from his porch.

A flash of memories from past decades... seventeen years old... running away to Texas...playing guitar all night in a smoky blues bar...parents crying... someone told them I'm probably dead.

I pull back on the yoke. The Cessna climbs through clouds above Saint Thomas. I should be in the airport rental office instead of doing aerial tricks, showing off for Marty and the kids over our house; the company owner went to Haiti to visit his girlfriend for the day.

Speeding along the autobahn, 120 mph, on a BMW R1200GS motorcycle...in the rain...suicidal mission? I often wondered through the years why I had survived. Why had I been kept alive?

Guilt...the pain of broken ideals...the voice of condemnation...

...An image flashes from the past: standing at the highest point in Paris on the hill of Montmartre, the smooth, flowing notes of a cellist reverberate from an alley across from the Sacra Coeur. Hymne a L'Amour (If You Love Me, Really Love Me). They were a mocking retort against the barrier of bitterness that had risen between us. Could love remove the pain? Or is the survival of a marriage actually the culmination of grit, discipline...perseverance?

We stood together...apart...listening...crying...her blond hair blowing in the wind...

Spinning…spinning…jumping in the waves off Upham Beach…

Earth to earth…nothing lasts…decay…doubt…questions….but now…what comes next?

I'm no longer spinning. My mind is at rest. I see the long tunnel with the white light at the end. Now nothing…?

\*TJ — Thomas J. Lentz, my son.
Laura — Laura Gage, my daughter
Selby — Selby Gage — my granddaughter
Tuula — Tuula Lentz — my granddaughter
Eeva — Eeva Lentz — my granddaughter
Marty — Marty Lentz — my wife

*The day a child realizes that all adults are imperfect, he becomes an adolescent. The day he forgives them, he becomes an adult. The day he forgives himself, he becomes wise…and can die in peace.*

Faith has not given me any absolute promise of an afterlife; but it has lessened my fear of the unknown. This life would have been easier with guarantees…with firm answers. I would have preferred a faith that could blot out the darkness.

I listen with heart-felt commiseration to the song for the sons of Korah… a petition to be saved from death:

*You have taken from me my closest friends…*
*…my eyes are dim with grief.*

*I call to you, Lord, every day…*
*…Are your wonders known in the place of darkness?*

*...I cry to you for help, Lord...*
*...Why, Lord, do you reject me,*
*And hide your face from me?*

*...darkness is my closest friend.*

(Excerpts from Psalm 88:14-18)

The Jewish carpenter cries out from a cross dripping with his blood:

*My God, why have you forsaken me?*

Can I profess to know more than they did? Should I expect more certainty?

I cannot suppress my curiosity. But I am skeptical of anyone who assumes to have more answers than this faithful psalmist or sinless prophet.

# Chapter 22

# Last Page

Marty, my steadfast wife of 53 years, asked me, "Why are you writing this? Who is your intended audience?" I don't know how to answer that. It's like asking, 'Why are you having a baby? What do you plan to do with him or her?' It happens; you start the process; and then you anticipate its arrival. It satisfies the longing to leave something behind: a testimony to your existence; something that has a life of its own.

The birth of a child is a nine month creative process for a woman. A father's participation is more abstract. Can the depth of his emotional connection equal that of motherhood? A father's involvement becomes more significant as the infant becomes a child who can walk and talk and reason. My son, Thomas Jeffrey, became my alter ego. In many respects I continue to live through him as I grow older.

When I traveled throughout Europe on a motorcycle several years ago, I often phoned my daughter at home in Ohio. She possesses the same nurturing instincts as her mother. She always seemed to be there to answer my calls. "It's so nice to know I can reach you at any time of night or day," I told her. "Yep," she said. "I never go anyplace. I'm always here with the two babies." Such is the life of devoted motherhood.

The three of them have tolerated my skepticism and have made my life worth living.

CPSIA information can be obtained
at www.ICGtesting.com
Printed in the USA
FFHW021208281218
50007181-54747FF

9 780788 040832